TALK LESS
listen more

solutions for children's
difficult behaviour

MICHAEL HAWTON

TALK LESS
listen more

solutions for children's
difficult behaviour

MICHAEL HAWTON

JCP

Talk Less, Listen More: Solutions for Children's Difficult Behaviour
By Michael Hawton
Published in 2013 by
Jane Curry Publishing 2013
[Wentworth Concepts Pty Ltd]
PO Box 780 Edgecliff NSW 2027 Australia
www.janecurrypublishing.com.au

National Library of Australia Cataloguing-in-Publication entry
Author: Hawton, Michael, author.
Title: *Talk less, listen more: solutions for children's difficult behaviour* /
           Michael Hawton.
ISBN: 9781922190697 (paperback)
ISBN: 9781922190710 (ebook: kindle)
ISBN: 9781922190703 (ebook: epub)
Subjects: Parenting--Popular works.
           Child rearing--Popular works.
           Child psychology--Popular works.
           Child development--Popular works.
Dewey Number: 649.64

Cover image: Shutterstock
Author photo: Jules Ober
Cover and internal design and layout: Melissa Keogh
Printed in Australia by McPherson's Printing Group

CONTENTS.

PART FIVE. EXTRA RESOURCES

preface

As your children grow, you'll probably want to concentrate on two main jobs at home. First, you'll want to consider their future, and figure out how to help them become the best people they can possibly be. Second, you'll want to make a difference to how they behave in situations here and now so that their behaviour is generally appropriate. This book provides you with a method for dealing with the difficult behaviour of children aged two to twelve years.

In *Talk Less, Listen More*, you'll learn that one of the main tasks of raising children is helping them assume better self-control. I draw from the latest findings in neuroscience — and describe these in language you will understand — offering strategies that will help you respond to your children when they misbehave. There are also cartoons, diagrams and worksheets to help you see what it 'looks like' when you're doing well. Have a flick through the book now and you'll see what I mean. Even though the family I use as an example is a nuclear one, with one father and one mother, the strategies here can be used by anyone who spends time caring for children, no matter what your particular family situation.

I suggest that you read this book from beginning to end simply because the method is more effective when you put some parts before others. Once you have laid down the foundations, you will find you have enough information to make quick and deliberate decisions. Having read this book, you should see yourself knowing what to do (and what not to do) next time your children look like they are misbehaving. You'll be able to respond more calmly to even the most difficult parenting situations. In time, I hope that you won't have to discipline your children so much, and will be able to enjoy them more.

I can't guarantee that what you're about to read is going to be comfortable for you and your children, but I hope it will give you a sense of confidence about what you're doing in managing your children's behaviour. I also hope that you will become more mindful of your decisions when you respond to your children if they are misbehaving. That's why most people seek help, by the way — because they get frustrated. You'll understand how to parent your children using some basic strategies that will have a big impact. These small actions will make a world of difference to your stress levels and the harmony of your family life.

Imagine, if you will, a most satisfying thought: wouldn't it be great if your kids grew up wanting to largely model, with their own children, the way you parented them? Well, it *can* be that way — you just need to know what to do, and to believe in yourself. Then you can get out there and get started. I hope this book will make it easier for you.

Michael Hawton.

what *Talk Less, Listen More* is all about

When I worked as a psychologist in a country town, three-quarters of the parents I saw lacked confidence in their ability to manage difficult behaviour. More often than not, they'd contacted our clinic because their children were misbehaving — either at school or at home. Some parents were stressed beyond belief. Some reckoned their children might have autism or ADHD, and sometimes they were right. Often they were tired of hearing themselves screaming at their kids. Many had 'hit the wall', having caught themselves walloping their child or doing something they found shocking: 'I smacked him the other day. It was all pretty crap, so I thought I'd better come along and do something about it.' As the saying goes, if I'd had a dollar for every time I heard that one, I'd be a rich man.

Other parents would come in saying, 'I don't want to be the kind of person who yells at their kids all the time.' Still others found themselves like the proverbial slow-boiling frog, gradually realising that things had become bad enough that they needed to seek help. Nearly all of them wondered if there was a better way of handling their children's problem behaviour.

I met many parents who wanted to move away from the things their parents had done. Some had experienced pretty harsh upbringings themselves and didn't want to repeat the mistakes their parents had made. (Inevitably, of course, we all make *some* of these mistakes, but I knew what they meant.) Some had a habit of losing their tempers when their kids misbehaved, so they just kept shouting at them because that was a familiar strategy.

After seeing parents struggling with the same problems over and over again, it dawned on me that they were probably happening not only in my community but in lots of towns and cities. Most parents were trying their best with what they knew; they hadn't set out to yell at or hit their children. Who would want to do that? They just didn't know what to do instead. They wanted solutions that were easy to understand and that would help them argue less with their children — clearly a very good motive for getting help. They didn't want control for the sake of control. And, whatever they learnt, I knew it had to also help their children become more resilient and happy in the long term.

So, I taught parents what I knew. We looked at the parts of their children's behaviour they could afford to ignore. We discussed how they could encourage their children by noticing what they were doing well. We talked about how they could show their children what they wanted them to do. I helped them understand how to be empathic and soothe emotional reactions by paying attention to their children's feelings. I gave them tip sheets and reading materials. I gave them homework. I modelled what they might do. We rehearsed how they might deal with repetitive problems, and how they might respond — calmly and effectively — next time their child was 'going off'. This slowly became what I thought of as the 'quiet parenting' method. Being quiet does not mean being silent, but it does mean using fewer words and not raising our voices as much.

WHAT CAN YOU ACHIEVE WITH THIS BOOK?

The feedback I received then, and have continued to receive after conducting hundreds of parent-training courses in person and online around the world, is that the *Talk Less, Listen More* strategies are easy to use in those stressful situations when your memory is often the first thing to go! Of course, when you're in a parenting jam, that's what you want — something that's easy to retrieve from your mind's eye.

While there will always be differences among children (and, for that matter, among parents) due to their genes or temperament, there are also lots of steps that will help them develop *self-control* — even if your little darling is somewhat on the wild side. What you will learn here is how to make better choices about your children's behaviour, whether that means limiting their behaviour when you need to, or promoting the behaviour you'd like to see repeated.

I offer a transition plan for moving your family from the state it is in now to one that is more harmonious. As you learn the systems in this book, you'll work out what to do in the most difficult parenting moments and to stop these challenging predicaments morphing into train wrecks. There are two main aims here: one, that your children will be able to assume better self-control; and two, that your family life will become calmer and much less stressful.

The best news I can give you is that it's not that hard. You just need a plan, and then to practise the essentials over and over until they become second nature to you in all situations.

HERE'S HOW THE BOOK IS ORGANISED

In **part 1** (chapters 1–4), we look at some broad brushstrokes for parenting: the main trends in parenting styles and research, some key principles, and the major mistakes parents tend to make when things get frantic at home. This is the first layer of understanding why our children behave as they do. By understanding these principles, even without knowing any of the later strategies, you'll change your situation at home — I promise.

In **part 2** (chapter 5), we look at change, and what's likely to happen when you first try to apply these new approaches. We investigate how you can deal with your children's resistance to change, and how you can keep yourself calm and focused — even if your children are not! By working out how change affects families, you can take steps to prepare yourself for any speed bumps that lie ahead.

In **part 3** (chapters 6–9), you'll learn about the choices you can make to manage your children's difficult behaviour — quietly. Here, you'll find out how you can help children get better at self-regulating, which means that they will be better behaved, without you having to remind them.

There are three main parenting choices: ignoring (actively overlooking behaviour); signalling (communicating to your child that you want them to stop what they are doing); and emotion coaching (empathising with a child to settle them). These will help you deal with here-and-now problems, while also helping children to practise key self-regulation skills.

In **part 4** (chapters 10–12), we explore some ways to promote the behaviour you want to see in your children, giving them life skills and an ability to maintain those skills. You may be surprised to find out that this isn't necessarily about using praise and rewards — which, in my opinion, are overused in some parenting approaches. I'll talk you through a process called PASTA that you can use with older children (ten years and up) that will help you deal with 'repeat offences'.

In **part 5**, you'll find some extra resources that may be helpful, including a worksheet — nothing scary! — so you can check your understanding of the main ideas in this book.

PART ONE.
trends, principles and mistakes

CHAPTER 1
trends in the field of parenting

In recent decades we've been taught that the best way to deal with behaviour problems is to talk them through with our children. While I'm not against this approach — it's one way of doing what needs to be done — the problem is that just talking doesn't always work. We've also been told what we *can't* do. We can't smack our children. We mustn't yell at them because it makes them cringe. We're not supposed to criticise them — the experts tell us it's bad for them. Some leaders in the field say we're not even meant to praise them, because it may mean that they only behave properly if we reward them.

As to how we *can* solve children's behaviour problems, though, it's pretty murky out there! There seem to be no clear solutions. We've become squeamish about putting limits on our children to stop them from behaving badly. Many of us feel judged by other parents, and this affects how we deal with difficult behaviour; we might not feel too good about pulling our children up for their behaviour, especially if others are watching.

POSITIVE PARENTING APPROACHES HAVE SOME LIMITATIONS

These days, we hear about 'positive parenting' approaches much more than the hard-line parental discipline of past eras. One parent I taught in a course suggested that we became accustomed to not giving our children boundaries when the cane was banned in the 1970s. Then we became insecure about containing our children's behaviour because we thought that somehow limiting them would harm them. Fast-forward a decade or so and families where both parents went out to work became more common, meaning that keeping on good terms with our children became important. One thing led to another and the fad of being 'friends' with our children emerged. And friends don't use discipline; it's not cool. Don't worry, I'm not suggesting that we step back to the 'children should be seen and not heard' days, but it's probably useful to consider the problem of managing our children's difficult behaviour from another angle.

I say this in an effort to understand why we have turned ourselves inside out as we constantly try to be positive with our children, even though most of *our* parents did not think this way. It's like we collectively agreed that we have to always be positive with our children in case they fall apart. Were the parents of previous generations deluded and ignorant because they didn't know how to parent positively? Or are *we* deluded by presuming that only positive parenting matters?

You see, I don't believe you always have to be positive with children to get a good outcome. And, importantly, I believe you can still maintain a close bond with your children even if you have to help them to contain their behaviour from time to time.

Let's look at a few examples of how we change behaviour in other areas. As a community, we have reduced the rate of smoking and, as a result, lung cancer. This is a good outcome, but it hasn't always been achieved via overtly positive messages for smokers. For example, most of us have seen TV advertisements where the message has been that smoking affects other people in our lives. This form of advertising works because, while you may not stop smoking for yourself, you may be more motivated to do it if it damages someone you love. Education, limitations (laws which say you can't smoke in restaurants), therapies (such as nicotine replacement) and taxes all go into the mix of strategies that reduce smoking. Another good example is the demerit points system used to sanction drivers who break traffic laws. Does this achieve positive results even though the means are not overtly positive? Many would argue that yes, it does: drivers realise that if they change their behaviour, they will keep the privilege of driving.

In my time, I have come across a wide range of parenting programs yet I haven't always been able to see a clear connection between what these programs offer and the needs of parents. It seems to me that most of the strategies on offer either instruct parents to talk about their expectations or to be 'positive' with their children. Somehow, the momentum has always been towards the positive. And if, as a parent, you aren't riding this positive wave, it seems you're doing the wrong thing.

In my years in psychology practice, seeing countless parents having difficulties with their children, it felt incredibly unhelpful to tell them they should just talk to their child about their behaviour, or even to put a positive spin on a child's outright rudeness or hurtfulness. In some situations, this is akin to suggesting that they put their proverbial thumbs in the dam wall. It just doesn't seem realistic to tell the parent of, say, a ten-year-old child who has been screaming and losing his temper for a long time to tell their son, 'Now, I want *you* to speak more calmly', when the child is routinely menacing his parents and siblings.

I am not saying 'positive parenting' approaches don't work to change behaviour in the long run. What I am saying is that most parents want solutions for addressing their children's behaviour problems *quickly*. Instead, the current research in child development and parenting clearly points to the benefits of a different approach: teaching children to successfully wrestle with their impulses, or to *self-regulate*. When children learn this early the research indicates that they will enjoy social and educational advantages throughout life. Study after study shows that children who learn to think before they act perform better in a whole range of social and educational situations. However, children do not necessarily learn self-regulation when parents focus only on positive behaviour. The challenge before us, as parents, is to learn to tolerate a bit of discomfort in our children to teach them these skills — at appropriate times. Only then will they learn how to be part of a family where things don't always go their way.

'OUTSIDE-IN' AND 'INSIDE-OUT' APPROACHES TO PARENTING

If we were to survey the kinds of parenting help available throughout the world, we'd find there are two main types of approaches: *outside-in* and *inside-out*.

Outside-in programs are those that teach parents to reward children for behaving in desirable ways. Parents teach children what is wanted, and make it obvious that they're 'pleased' with what their children are doing. Unwanted behaviour is then discouraged through sanctions, consequences, withdrawing privileges or punishment. The main leverage point in sanctioning children's behaviour is that something unpleasant or uncomfortable occurs to 'teach' them this behaviour is unacceptable. This approach relies on a parent behaving in a certain way to change their children's behaviour. The generally accepted view held by professionals who teach outside-in strategies is that they work best if more positive strategies than negative ones are used.

So, the outside-in theory goes something like this. If we want children to behave more co-operatively, we need to show them *how* to behave, and teach them, encourage them and build bonds with them. If certain behaviour is expected and expected consistently, we should be able to improve it by teaching it — and by offering incentives. The ratio of positives to negatives should be in the order of five to one.

We will discuss some of the limitations of 'outside-in' — reward and punishment — strategies in later chapters. For the moment, we're going to look at another type of parenting approach: promoting children's abilities from the 'inside-out'.

Inside-out strategies focus on how we can help children pay attention to their feelings and then manage those feelings. These strategies hold that by teaching children about their emotional software and how it works, we can increase their emotional flexibility. The aim of inside-out parenting strategies is to help children operate their emotional 'accelerators' and 'brakes'. Children learn how to recognise their feelings, even if momentarily, and then catch themselves before acting on their emotions.

When all is said and done, the task of parenting probably requires us to use a bit of both of these approaches. This requires us to use different strategies (not too many) depending on the different behaviours we see — so we can 'discourage' unwanted behaviour and 'promote' the behaviour we want to see.

WHERE DOES DIFFICULT BEHAVIOUR COME FROM?

The first thing that needs to be said about children's difficult behaviour is that, more often than not, it's an *emotional* overreaction. Although our children don't necessarily see it that way, we do. If you look at children behaving poorly, it's clear that:

1. they are very emotional

2. they just don't know what to do to manage their emotions.

A flare-up may start as a small feeling but turn into something bigger that is expressed as yelling or getting angry. Think of twelve-year-old Tom, who gets mad with his mother for not letting him go to his friend's place; seven-year-old Matty, who speaks rudely to his dad when prevented from hurting his little sister; or five-year-old Jessica, who tries to hit her beloved grandmother, Nonna Bartoli (you'll meet her soon), because Nonna has told her she can't have a biscuit before dinner. Children's difficult behaviour nearly always begins from an emotional base, and goes up from there.

Part of growing up is developing an ability to control our strong feelings. One writer who has attempted to define what it is to 'grow up' is Scott Peck. In the 1970s, Peck wrote a book called *The Road Less Travelled* in which he described how we mature as adults and what we would be doing if we were fully mature. Essentially, he demonstrated that developing maturity is partly about how well we balance our emotions in proportion to our experiences:

- If I think someone has given me the wrong change at a shop, just how upset should I get?

- If someone pushes ahead of me at the bus stop, just how annoyed should I be?

- If I'm a child and my father tells me I can't do something, just how frustrated should I become?

Let's take one of these as an example. Imagine someone barges in ahead of you while you're lined up to catch a bus. In the greater scheme of things, this event may be a 4/10 event and probably deserves a 4/10 emotional response. Depending on how you see it, though, it may evoke an 8/10 anger response. A different event, such as a threat to a member of your family, may be a 9/10 event that triggers a 9/10 reaction: a level of reaction that may be entirely appropriate. There is a relationship between the event and the emotional reaction. More often than not, the two should be *in balance*.

As adults, of course, we make judgments about how to respond in social situations all the time. We make frequent decisions about whether or not someone is impinging on our mental or physical space. It's a normal part of everyday life to make these judgments so other people do not take advantage of us. As adults, we've developed sophisticated social antennae to pick up on variations in the way people behave towards us that help us decide how to react. Essentially, these 'feelers' help us work out if a person is going to be friendly or not. What we may initially see as unfriendly behaviour may not be that at all and, depending on the circumstances, we can change our view quite quickly and act accordingly. For example, we might come to the conclusion that a person has made an innocent mistake, or at least see *why* they did something we don't agree with.

Children experience their own frustrations, but because their brains are still developing they interpret events differently. What children interpret as 'frustrating' may not be apparent to an adult. Working out what's really frustrating and what's not can be a tough ask when you're a child. Clearly, not every situation is a 9/10 event, but what we often see in children who behave poorly is a disproportionate reaction to something as innocuous as a 'Later ...' or a 'Not now ...' from a parent. The children I have seen who have marked behaviour problems have often developed a pattern of letting their emotions fly. They haven't learnt how to manage their strong feelings, or pull back from the emotional brink.

I believe that our children's ability to harness their feelings depends partly on their stage of development (meaning that we would expect them to develop this ability as they get older) and partly on learning the skills to deal with their frustration. And they *can* learn these skills. Given the right circumstances, I firmly believe that we can improve children's ability to self-regulate.

IT'S IMPORTANT FOR CHILDREN TO LEARN SELF-REGULATION

When I was learning my profession, a psychiatrist-supervisor told me that, in his experience, most children's behaviour problems are to do with self-regulation. What he meant was that children with behaviour problems usually haven't figured out how to control their feelings. This insight has stayed with me for a long time, and has been supported by my own professional experience. You see, except for a small number of people (such as those with brain problems or personality disorders), nearly everyone, including our children, has some ability to 'catch' themselves before they lose control of their feelings. The problem is that even if we have this ability, we may not always use it.

Let me give you some examples of children I worked with during my time as a psychologist in practice. Because I was a male psychologist, a lot of boys were sent my way, and I interviewed many aged ten to thirteen with difficult behaviour. Their parents hoped that someone could teach their boys how to control their tempers. Many of them were referred because their parents or teachers saw them losing control at home or at school — usually by hitting or being aggressive.

As I got to talking with them, they told me that most of the time they were aware of their frustration. They knew their anger was there but, instead of learning to control their feelings, they'd formed a bit of habit of just letting rip. In many cases, the problem appeared to be that they didn't know *how* to control their angry feelings. They either didn't see that they had a choice to calm down, or they just became angry because that's what they did out of habit. They weren't able to access a reflective space in themselves where they could 'get a grip'. No wonder they got into lots of trouble!

The funny thing was that when I asked them if they wanted to learn how to stop themselves from getting so angry, they usually said 'Yes'. Their tempers got them into trouble, you see. Their problem was they didn't know *how* to do it. I'd ask, 'When you're in the situation you've been telling me about, and you're beginning to *feel* upset, is there a moment when you can sense you are getting angrier? Can you feel a time when you're going to get even angrier? You know, when your anger is going to get bigger?' Again, they said, 'Well … yeah.' They *knew* their feelings were getting more intense, but they hadn't worked out how to pull back and control them. They tended to let a small amount of anger get bigger, rather than harnessing it.

I knew that if they could notice when they were getting angrier, they stood a chance of managing their anger. Often, once the boys learnt to notice their angry feelings, we worked out what to do about them. However, unless they could accurately identify their feelings it was impossible to learn to control them.

WHAT IS THE ROLE OF THE BRAIN IN SELF-REGULATION?

We now know there's a special part of the brain that controls our feelings in interpersonal situations. It sits just behind our foreheads. It's called the *pre-frontal cortex* and, as we develop and mature, it plays a big role in limiting our behaviour in tricky encounters. But it needs nurturing to work properly. We can help it develop in our children by teaching them to pay the right attention to it. In his book *The Brain that Changes Itself*, psychiatrist Norman Doidge highlights the role of the pre-frontal cortex by looking at what happens when it is *not* very active — when we're asleep. During sleep, we experience increased activity in the part of our brains that processes emotion, producing vivid sexual, survival and aggressive dreams. Our impulses are amplified but are not held in check by the pre-frontal cortex.

So when we are talking about parenting and helping children control their behaviour, we ignore the role of the pre-frontal cortex at our peril. I know it may sound overly simplistic to emphasise a very small (but very important) part of the brain, but our ability to regulate our emotions is there. It's there that our ability to pause and catch ourselves lies, as well as our ability to restrain ourselves long enough to figure out what to do in stressful social encounters, to decide whether we should act or show restraint. For our children to develop self-regulation, it is essential that we help foster these abilities.

How you raise your children *does* affect how the pre-frontal cortex develops. For better or for worse, what happens in our children's environment has some effect on what happens in their brains. Incoming information — signals, words, noise, smells, touch, affection and care — all influence how the brain organises itself. The pre-frontal area is the place in which the brain achieves self-organisation. If we can help our children exercise the neurons in the pre-frontal cortex, we can help them strengthen their brain's organising ability and moderate their urge to act on their impulses. Their moral code is in this part of their brains; it helps them determine right from wrong.

A simple way to think about your job as a parent is to consider your role as similar to that of a personal trainer in a 'mind gym'. If you can give your children important tips to focus their attention on the part of the brain that helps them be more flexible in social circumstances, you're thinking along the right lines. By coaching like this, you should see them take greater control over their urges. The outcome will be a child who is not only better behaved but, having noticed their emotions, more able to self-regulate.

CHILDREN'S BRAINS HAVE BRAKES AND ACCELERATORS

Children are generally not as good as adults at using their mental 'brakes' as they are at using their mental 'accelerators'. The pre-frontal cortex which inhibits their responses has not fully developed. In addition, children who regularly misbehave are usually really good at using their mental 'accelerators', but not so good at using their mental 'brakes'. What paediatricians and psychologists notice about children presenting with difficult behaviour is that they *look* out of control. They're not able to limit themselves. For example, one pre-school teacher I know had to sit next to a wayward charge — with her hand on the child's hand — to prevent the child flicking paint on to the child next to her. This lack of control can appear to be a purely emotional reaction — not filtered by any rational process and certainly not considering any consequences. When we say about someone, 'They're losing it', the 'it' we're referring to is the ability to control feelings.

We'll look at this more closely in a moment, and see an example of what happens when children only use their accelerators. To do that, though, we'll need to introduce our 'host' family, the Blooms, who you'll meet throughout this book.

meet the Bloom family

Here are Serena and Charlie Bloom. They have three children: Tom, twelve; Matty, seven; and Jessica, five. Here is also Maria Bartoli, Serena's mother. Nonna Bartoli is at the Blooms' house on a regular basis and has a lot to do with her grandchildren. She's more than passionate about them.

Charlie and Serena met fourteen years ago. Charlie's had a few jobs — he's been a bank teller and a carpenter, and now he's a sales rep who spends a bit of time on the road. Serena works part-time at a computer software company and is secretly competitive about her family. Charlie was the boy she dreamed about at school, and they married thirteen years ago.

The Blooms may or may not be like families you know, but 'typical' families are very hard to pinpoint these days. What you'll notice, though, is that they face many of the problems most families face, and you should find the strategies we discuss should work for you, too.

The Blooms love their children dearly, but they've had their difficulties. At the moment, they're having the most difficulty with Matty, their middle child, and have had to outsource for help. Their GP has sent them off to a paediatrician, Dr Catherine Wiles, to see if Matty is OK, or if he needs some kind of special assistance.

Throughout this book, we'll see how Serena and Charlie learn parenting tips from Dr Wiles as she helps them manage Matty's behaviour.

IN CHILDREN, THE ABILITY TO SHOW RESTRAINT GETS BETTER AND BETTER

 Matty Bloom is a boy with underdeveloped brakes. Charlie and Serena know he's not really a naughty boy, but they are not sure what to do about him. At their first interview with Dr Wiles, they report that Matty's been behaving like a 'cheeky monkey' for some months. He's become a bit of a tearaway and Serena, especially, is really struggling keeping it together. At home, Matty often gets furious at his parents if they try to limit what he does. He has no patience with his younger sister, Jessica, and regularly lets loose at her. He's often rude to those around him. Too often Serena finds herself shouting at Matty when he refuses to do as he's told.

Anyone observing Matty would see his behaviour being played out in the following ways:

- he yells a lot

- he is often defiant

- he gets easily exasperated when things don't go his way

- he often pesters his parents

- he has a limited ability to stop himself from becoming outright defiant.

A key question about Matty's behaviour is whether or not he can be taught the skills to take control of himself. Serena and Charlie tell Dr Wiles that in some situations — such as when Matty's at school — he can exercise a degree of self-control. But at home it's a different story. As a result, the Blooms are exhausted. Every time they attempt to limit Matty's behaviour, he becomes frustrated or loses his temper.

So, what could be happening in Matty's mind? It's best illustrated by a related story involving an adult who is a little better at dealing with frustration than Matty. Most adults have a way of regulating their emotions I call *toggling*, and here's how it works.

TOGGLING IN ACTION: A RUGBY GAME

Picture the scene: the Australian Wallabies are playing the New Zealand All Blacks in a rugby union decider at Suncorp Stadium in Queensland. The score is 22–20 in Australia's favour, and there's five minutes to go before full time. A roaring crowd of 50,000 people watches the thrilling final minutes, with tens of thousands more glued to their TV screens across Australia and New Zealand.

The All Blacks have won a scrum feed close to the Australian line. The sides pack down and the scrum quickly buckles up as the packs push against each other. Almost immediately one of the All Blacks' second rowers, number 5, throws a punch through the middle of the scrum, hitting his opposite number in the face.

The Wallabies' forward hits back, and a fight breaks out. Punches fly left and right, and there seem to be at least fifteen players, from both sides, involved in the ruckus.

When the fighting stops, the referee listens to the linesmen's reports. He nods his head in understanding. The linesmen leave the field and the referee calls for the Australian number 5 to come to him. According to the linesmen, it appears the Australian player threw the first punch. The referee sternly admonishes the player and is about to award a penalty that will probably result in Australia losing the match.

For this young man, it's a very emotional event. He knows that if the All

Blacks get the penalty, Australia's likely to lose. He's furious. After all, he didn't start the fight and yet he's the one being penalised. His chest is heaving and his brow is furrowed as he stands before the referee like a steaming six-foot-four ogre. He's outraged that he's been singled out.

This player is angry, and his mind is going at a thousand miles an hour, trying to work stuff out. One part of his brain is experiencing pretty wild things. It's saying, 'Hit the ref! Let him have it! Spray this guy!' This emergency part of his brain — we can call this his 'old brain' — is reacting big time to what's going on. It doesn't necessarily see reason — it just reacts.

But as we watch the player's face we can see something happening: his eyes dart from left to right and back again. In another part of his brain, just behind his forehead — in the pre-frontal cortex, in fact — there are neurons firing, helping him keep control. As mentioned earlier, this is the part of our brains that has developed over many thousands of years to help us exert emotional control in stressful social situations. It's what we might call his 'new brain', and it's sending him other messages: 'Don't hit ref. Lifetime suspension. Take it on the chin …'

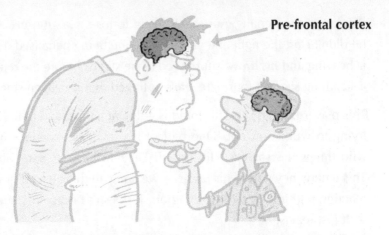

He knows that it's *not* OK for him to strike the referee, and he will face serious consequences if he does. Despite his anger, he maintains control, and swallows the referee's decision without losing his grip on the situation.

The footballer is able to wrestle with his impulses; he is an adult, after all. So, what is the mechanism that has equipped this player to take charge of his strong feelings? It's an important question to ask, because this mechanism is at the seat of all children's misbehaviour — *all* of it. Matty Bloom will learn more about it as he gets older, but he can also improve his capacity to do it with some help from his parents. I call this process of shifting back and forth between the different parts of the brain *toggling*.

TOGGLING ALLOWS US TO SUCCESSFULLY WRESTLE WITH STRONG EMOTION

Toggling is the process by which we trade 'old brain' information with 'new brain' information. The footballer is toggling back and forth, back and forth, between the part of his brain that wants to explode and the part of his brain that is capable of containing his anger. At lightning-fast speeds he is wrestling with competing signals as one part of his brain wants to erupt while another part, reading the social situation, realises it's not the best time to lose control. His pre-frontal cortex is working, telling him to hold; it's not worth being sent off, and who knows, the other team might miss scoring a goal with their free kick.

You and I have faced this kind of situation — where we experience a tricky interpersonal moment and limit ourselves. We still feel upset but, somehow, we're able to keep on top of our feelings and do it effectively enough to behave appropriately on most occasions. If you've ever watched *The Simpsons*, you'll have seen Homer Simpson toggling; it happens when he's under stress and his eyes dart back and forth as he tries to work out what he'll do next. This toggling is less developed in children than it is in adults. Even so, it's still present in children as young as four. Now, isn't toggling a skill we want to see our own children use?

Serena and Charlie have already told Dr Wiles that Matty *can* stop himself from overreacting at certain times. All they need to do is help him practise this skill if he is to get better at regulating his own behaviour. At the moment, Matty has two things working against him: his brain has not fully matured, and he has not been practising the skills he needs to learn to do this. But Matty's parents can accelerate this ability by teaching him how to use it, just as they can teach him to add numbers together or ride a bicycle.

TOGGLING IS A LEARNABLE MENTAL SKILL

In my experience, children with behaviour problems often suffer 'brain-lock'. They don't know how to be flexible and change tack. They get rigid or fixed when faced with a limit, and their difficult behaviour tends to escalate. Matty Bloom has developed such a habit. I used to see a lot of 'Mattys' in my waiting room.

Toggling reflects how one part of our brain can wrestle control over another part in high-stakes situations. By practising, can a child improve this ability? Neuroscience researchers have discovered that when certain clusters of neurons in our brains are used, and reused, the clusters become stronger. This is important news and it has a big bearing on how we parent. Studies have shown that the parts of the brain that control escalation *do* improve if they are used more often. In other words, the part of the brain that allows for flexibility can be made to work better. We just need to help children focus their attention.

This is kind of weird, but true. It means that if we can help a child like Matty practise switching between his accelerators and his brakes, the neurons that filter 'braking' in his brain will work better. In Matty's case, helping him to not lose control — which he has grown used to doing — will not only largely fix his behaviour problems, but should also help him self-regulate in the long term. By practising toggling, some psychologists and psychiatrists say, he will grow the 'muscles' in that part of his brain that will help him take control of his feelings.

We want Matty to be able to successfully harness certain feelings so that he does not get overwhelmed by them. At the moment this is his major problem. Not only is he unable to pull himself up when he has gone too far, but he is also developing a belief that he is entitled to have as much say as his mum or dad about what he can do. His view is that he doesn't have to pull back when he feels like escalating.

His parents need to show him that it's better to learn to cope with all sorts of feelings. They can teach him to get better at *wrestling* with his feelings, to successfully pause, and '*um*' and '*er*' before he loses his cool. In time he will learn that some restraint makes his life more comfortable and he gets into trouble less often.

REMEMBER THAT FEELINGS ARE IMPORTANT

There's no denying that we're all entitled to our feelings. We expect that our children will express lots of feelings during their lives; that's essential. That's not what we are talking about here. It's very important for parents to help children name and experience their feelings so that they learn not to be frightened by them. But, equally, a part of maturing is learning how to keep our feelings in proportion to events. If Matty's parents are to help him to have better control of himself, they'll need to help him understand what happens, in himself, when he experiences feelings.

Appropriate social behaviour is not just about the expression or non-expression of our feelings; it is also about *how* those feelings are expressed. Over time, we all learn how to live in a family or a group where we have obligations to one another. When it comes to our children, we don't want them to automatically go berserk when they are pulled up for their misbehaviour. Sometimes, yes, it's understandable, but more often than not it's just not OK. And, frankly, there are times when we have to give instructions to our children without having them question us. The time will come for them to be independent, but that time has not arrived when they are still only seven years old.

It's not that we want Matty to never get angry. He will. Indeed, there are times when he should, if merely to learn how to stand up for himself. However, there are times when we all need to limit our reactions and manage our feelings.

WHAT KIND OF PRACTICE DO CHILDREN NEED TO SELF-REGULATE?

To teach Matty to wrestle with his feelings successfully, his parents need to provide him with the right kind of practice. This involves doing certain things in a certain order. It's the job of Serena and Charlie to set limits on his inappropriate behaviour by giving him cues to help him with his internal ability to self-regulate.

Another illustration will help show how these self-control mechanisms work and, importantly, how we can promote them in our children.

IT'S ALL ABOUT RESISTING THE MARSHMALLOW...

In the 1960s Walter Mischel, a psychologist from Stanford University, conducted some experiments to test the ability of four-year-old children to control their impulses. The experiment (conducted with about 650 children) went like this. First, a four-year-old was asked to sit down in front of a plate with one marshmallow on it. The researcher then said that they (i.e. the researcher) would leave the room for fifteen minutes. If the child did *not* eat the marshmallow in that time, they would get a second marshmallow when the researcher returned. If the child *did* eat it, there would be no second one offered. The researcher then left.

These children were facing a mental challenge. They could eat the marshmallow now, or hold off for the possibility of a reward of *two* marshmallows: a tough ask if you're four! (For some adults, this would be like having to wait for two hours for that first coffee in the morning.) Lots of children grimaced or smelled the marshmallow but didn't give in. Some hummed, or looked the other way. Some scrunched their faces. Some tapped their feet or waited impatiently. These were the children who could delay eating the marshmallow. When the researcher returned fifteen minutes later, they received the second marshmallow, as promised.

Mostly, though, the children ate the marshmallow within fifteen minutes. They couldn't wait. They often couldn't keep their eyes off the marshmallow. At four most of them could *not* control their impulses.

Mischel's results were that:

- two-thirds of children (the 'grabbers') were not able to resist the marshmallow and ate it

- one-third of children (the 'delayers') were able to wait, and subsequently received a second marshmallow.

When the children he had studied were teenagers, Mischel found some startling trends among them. He found that the children who had been able to resist grew into teenagers with better abilities. They were more persistent, had greater social abilities and did better at school than the children who could not wait for fifteen minutes when they were four years old. The children who could not wait had more health problems and were more likely to have behaviour problems.

So Mischel asked the question: what was the difference between the two groups? Was one set of children psychologically healthier? Did one group have a better bond with their parents and were they therefore more secure? Were they more trusting that the second marshmallow would show up as promised?

One explanation that makes sense to many psychologists who have studied this experiment is that the children who were able to resist had learnt something about shifting their attention. That is, instead of latching onto the desire to eat the one marshmallow in front of them, they had learnt to fade their attention away from a temptation and focus on something else.

Were these children like the rugby player who successfully wrestled with, and avoided giving into, his initial fury? Were some children, even at four years of age, able to tolerate having a strong urge (i.e. to eat) and yet not satisfy it immediately?

Clearly, some young children can toggle between their 'old brain' messages and their 'new brain' messages.

WE *CAN* TEACH CHILDREN TO RESIST THE MARSHMALLOW

So, if the four-year-olds who were 'delayers' did much better educationally and socially when they were teenagers, is there any way to help the 'grabbers'? Can we teach children to grapple with their strong emotions or shift their attention? Well, it appears we can. Follow-up marshmallow studies by psychologist Albert Bandura showed that it is possible to teach the 'grabbers' to limit their impulses by redirecting their attention.

Bandura put children who were initially grabbers in contact with an adult role model who could demonstrate waiting by shifting their attention to something else. By watching adult role models, these children were taught to wait, and learnt how to distract themselves. They observed the adults placing their heads down for a nap, humming, looking away or engaging in some other distracting experience. Some months later, these children were shown to have largely retained this ability. They had *learnt* techniques to keep their minds off a temptation.

This is significant because it means that self-regulation is not a fixed characteristic, as Mischel had first supposed; it is something that, with some practice, can be learnt. To get better at delaying, you just have to learn what to do! Bandura's experiments showed that we can teach children to focus on an alternative activity instead of giving into a here-and-now urge. So, if we say that a lot of 'difficult behaviour' in children is an *emotional reaction* gone awry, we need to ask whether or not we can better equip these children to resist acting on impulse. I believe we can, if we teach them to toggle and then self-regulate. (For a very funny rendition of this experiment, see the Joachim de Posada web link in the 'Further reading and resources' section.)

LEARNING THE SKILLS OF EMOTIONAL INTELLIGENCE HELPS CHILDREN SELF-REGULATE

The American psychologist and author Daniel Goleman says there are some key steps to learning emotional control. If we can help our children *identify* their feelings — by listening empathically to them and helping them label their emotions — they will be more able to self-regulate. Children who are immersed in a family culture in which feelings are valued learn to manage their emotions better than those in situations in which their feelings are not honoured. Importantly, though, honouring children's *feelings* does not mean we should accept all their *behaviour*.

In his book *Emotional Intelligence*, Goleman says that emotional-regulation skills are only gained in a certain order, and start with children identifying feelings and then learning words to match how they feel. This means we can help our children reflect on their emotions by showing them how to name their feelings. This first skill of 'noticing' feelings is a prerequisite for learning the later skills of 'tracking' and 'managing' Tracking means being able to feel something but not necessarily react to it — you just experience it.

CHILDREN NEED TO EXPERIENCE SOME DISCOMFORT TO LEARN SELF-REGULATION

The idea of intentionally placing our children into uncomfortable situations and helping them improve their wrestling with tricky emotions does not sit well with many of us. But while it's natural to want our children to be happy all the time, we cannot shield them from all discomfort. The reality is that children need small doses of focused discomfort if they are to learn to cope with situations that require them to use their mental brakes. We're not talking about abusive discomfort here but, rather, discomfort that teaches our children a skill. Remember, the children who could wait for the second marshmallow had learnt something that helped them not act on impulse — even though it was *uncomfortable* to do so. They had learnt to tolerate a certain amount of frustration for a greater reward. In this case, some discomfort equals a better reward, but no discomfort equals a lesser reward.

A more worrying concern is that the children who don't practise grappling with strong feelings won't develop the connections in their brains to help them work their mental brakes. If children don't have experiences that help them tolerate discomfort, such as having their parents set a limit, they may not develop the mental capacity to operate their brakes. As psychiatry professor Daniel Siegel says: it's in the mental wrestling with strong feelings that children develop flexibility. In other words, without practise in putting their foot on the brake pedal from time to time, children will never acquire the mental brake 'shoes' they need. In the worst cases, emotionally immature children and young people will never learn to limit their feelings and will be much more likely to end up in trouble. Often, children with marked behaviour problems have never improved their ability to wrestle with strong feelings when they need to. No practice, see?

Like any skill, children need to learn the skill of self-regulation from someone like a coach … or a parent. That's where you come in. Next, we'll look more closely at how children's brains grow and develop, and show you some pretty concrete examples of how children can misunderstand situations or see things from another perspective.

in essence

- There is a range of *parenting approaches*; one is the 'positive' parenting style. On its own, this has some limitations in dealing with children's behaviour problems.

- *Outside-in* approaches to parenting reward children for desirable behaviour and sanction or punish children for undesirable behaviour. *Inside-out* strategies, on the other hand, aim to help children notice and manage their feelings and behaviour. Parents need to work on these two fronts at the same time.

- Difficult behaviour in children usually begins with an *emotional overreaction*. Encouraging emotional skills in children, where we teach them to gain control over their feelings, is therefore an important part of parenting.

- The *pre-frontal cortex* is the part of the brain that gives us our ability to regulate our emotions. It develops as children grow older.

- We want our children to learn to wrestle with their emotions — to *toggle* — so they strengthen the flexibility of their pre-frontal cortex.

- Parents can teach children to use their *mental brakes*, but children need to experience some discomfort to learn self-regulation. If they don't practise grappling with strong feelings, they won't develop the connections in their brains to help them appropriately pause and catch themselves.

- Waiting for a second marshmallow is better than eating one now!

CHAPTER 2
children's development and behaviour

When our now-adult daughter was about four, my wife and I were building a fence at the back of our home while she rode her tricycle nearby. Out of the blue she said, 'I want lunch!' Her mother called back to her (while holding up a fence railing at one end), 'We'll get lunch soon. Daddy and I are busy right now.'

'I want lunch!' she proclaimed again. I remember turning to her and saying that we couldn't get lunch just then, but we would soon. Then, another louder demand: 'I want *lunch*!' By this time, we were ignoring her requests, knowing that once we had the final fence rail up we could tend to her. There was a moment of silence until suddenly she shouted, 'I WANT *LUNCH*! I WANT IT *NOW*! If you DON'T get me lunch, when you're OLD, I'm not going to FEED you!'

We got lunch soon after this.

Children's ability to understand and balance their emotions is closely related to their stage of development. With increasing age comes an increasing control over impulses and moods. When children are little, though, they're more dependent on other people — such as their parents — to help them understand their feelings. As they mature they become more self-dependent.

CHILDREN'S ABILITIES ARE DETERMINED BY THEIR STAGE OF DEVELOPMENT

As children move through the stages of development, you will see gradual improvements in their ability to self-regulate. No matter how smart they appear to be, though, it's important to remember that their capacity for controlling their emotions is related to their developmental stage. So, let's have a brief look at some of these limitations and how they apply to children of different ages.

TWELVE-MONTH-OLDS COMMUNICATE USING SOUNDS AND GESTURES TO GET WHAT THEY WANT

At this age, these grunts are sometimes accompanied by arm movements. These gestures and sounds work in the absence of words, because the expressive language parts of the brain are still to develop.

Toddlers often use their sounds and gestures to get us to notice what they want. Once, at an airport, I watched a toddler who was about fourteen months old. Her grandmother was standing above her. She pulled at her gran's trousers, repeated 'Neneh! Neneh', lifted both her arms up, and opened and closed her hands, clearly showing that she wanted to be picked up. Her grandmother did as she wished: she leaned over and picked her up. 'Wow, that's how it works,' I thought.

Without an adult's empathy, this type of communication would not work. We have learnt to survive by taking advantage of this form of communication, reinforced because it works to get our needs met.

Even though the part of a toddler's brain that produces words (known as Broca's area) hasn't yet fully developed, the part of the brain that can think (known as Wernicke's area) is open for business. In toddlers, Wernicke's area has developed to the point where it can work out what it wants. In a few years Broca's area will have caught up, but for most toddlers the grunt or single sound (which, from my experience, reappears in many teenagers) will do the job, thank you very much! So, the part of a toddler's brain that can figure out what it *needs* is functioning just fine, but the child relies on a close connection with others — mum, dad, other trusted people — to *get* what they want. Holophrases, as they are called, bridge the communication gap between a toddler and the outside world. An empathic bond, formed through attachment, enables the adult to know how to respond.

As children develop, their brains grow from the back area to the front area where decisions are made. Unfortunately, very young children cannot do the mental tasks that older children (or adults) can do, including controlling their impulses. So what may appear a reasonable request by us may appear outrageous to a three-year-old. This means that they may appear to be more inflexible, and to have a lower tolerance for frustration, than adults. Frustration tolerance is an ability that continues to grow all the way through childhood.

Children get better at reasoning as they mature.

Reasoning, too, improves as children mature, but is limited in younger children, as the experiments of Jean Piaget (described below) show.

JEAN PIAGET'S EXPERIMENTS

To show how the nature of children's thinking changes as they grow older, French psychologist Jean Piaget did a number of experiments.

In one, with four-year-old children, he put the same amount of liquid into two containers of the same shape and size. He then moved the liquid into two new, different-sized containers and assessed the children's responses.

Here are the original containers: both hold the same amount of liquid. Piaget asked the children if the containers held the same amount of liquid. Most children agreed they did.

Piaget then poured all the liquid from the two original containers into a taller and thinner container. He asked the children again if the containers held the same amount of liquid.

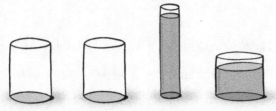

Piaget's findings were repeated many times. Here's what he found. Children aged three to four — no matter how intelligent they were — *nearly always* thought the amount of liquid increased when it was shifted from the original container to the taller container. Even though they had watched the same amount of liquid being poured from the original containers into both the taller and squatter containers they believed that the taller, thinner container held more. The children *could not* understand that the amount of liquid remained the same.

Why is this? Well, the part of children's brains that organises this level of complexity is still developing in four-year-olds. At five, children are increasingly able to keep the image of the same amount of liquid 'alive' in their minds. This ability to remember and connect information is a hallmark of a more sophisticated ability that children gain at their next stage of cognitive development.

Food manufacturers, by the way, use this illusion to great advantage. Ever noticed how the taller, thinner jars in the supermarket look like they hold more than the shorter, wider ones?

FIVE-YEAR-OLD-CHILDREN ARE NORMALLY VERY SELF-CENTRED

All over the world, five-year-old children are not very good at sharing. This is because they are at their most egocentric age. They usually grow out of it but we, as adults, can get frustrated when they appear not to think of others. Some parents don't understand this stage and want their children to be good at sharing with other children. But five-year-olds are just not built for taking turns or divvying things up. It's not in their make-up. However, with time, growth and encouragement they can get better at this.

NINE-YEAR-OLDS HAVE A CONCEPT OF 'FAIRNESS'

By the age of nine, children enter a stage where many things are a moral dilemma. They can't work out what to do because they want to be fair all the time. Nine-year-olds are well known for speaking in terms of moral imperatives. In their minds, they say, 'If it is like this for *one* person, it should be like this for the *other* person.' So: 'He sat in the front last time; it's my turn to sit in the front' or 'You're not being fair!' are common complaints.

This belief in fairness is the mantra of nine-year-olds. At a high-school drama production recently, I sat next to a nine-year-old and we struck up a conversation. I asked which act she liked best (I had some favourites I thought I'd share with her). She said, 'I liked them all!' What else should I have expected? Of course she liked them all — she wanted to be fair!

TWELVE-YEAR-OLDS CAN THINK IN RELATIVE TERMS

Twelve-year-old children, though, are better at thinking in less absolute terms. They can say to themselves, 'It may not be fair today, but my sister is sick so she can have an extra turn. Tomorrow, I'll sit in the front.'

THE BRAIN KEEPS DEVELOPING THROUGHOUT CHILDHOOD AND ADOLESCENCE

As children grow older, their mental machinery becomes more agile. Children's minds become more *developed*, allowing them to deal with increasing levels of complexity.

As far as parenting is concerned, it's good to know what we can reasonably expect of our children at different ages. There are simply going to be times when they will find it hard to follow our reasoning or agree with us. This difference between the way *they* see things and the way *we* see things can cause big problems. Of course, this is not to say that children are not intelligent, but merely to point out that, in developmental terms, they've got some way to go before they can fully understand our way of looking at the world. After all, they're not 'mini-me's'.

SO, WHAT IS HAPPENING INSIDE THEIR HEADS?

At three years of age, children's heads are, on average, eighty per cent of their adult size. By six years of age, a child's head is nearly ninety per cent of its adult size. So it's no wonder we look at our children and say, 'Your head is as big as mine, so why don't you get what I'm saying to you?' With their almost-adult head size, it seems reasonable to think our children should know more than they do, or even to think they should know the things *we* know. But looking at our children from the outside cannot tell us what's going on inside.

Even though our children may speak and behave like adults at times, inside their brains they are constantly growing neural pathways — all the way through to full adulthood. We say to ourselves: 'He sounds so grown-up; maybe he *does* know what he's talking about.' But inside every child's brain, connections are still being made. With a microscope you can see individual neurons move around and seek each other out. These brain fibres dance and are attracted to one another — like something out of a sci-fi movie — as they search for and make connections with other neurons. Crazy, huh?

One way of thinking about the limitations of children's brains is to imagine five or six computers that, from the outside, all look the same. However, inside the casings they have very different capacities. Some are more sophisticated and have more hardware, more software and more memory. Some can do more things than others. It's hard, though, to tell this by looking at their casings. You have to investigate each one before making any assumptions based on how they look. As with our children, *understanding* what's inside is the only way to work out what they can and can't do.

THE PRE-FRONTAL AREAS OF THE BRAIN DEVELOP UNTIL WE ARE IN OUR TWENTIES

The pre-frontal areas of our brains play a very important part in our development. These areas help us make judgments, draw conclusions and plan for the future. Over time they help us to organise information, but they do not entirely finish growing until we reach our mid-twenties. In the following illustrations, you can see how there is a 'forest' of connections being made between neurons that result in more and more sophistication and a greater ability to solve problems.

Physical growth of the cortex

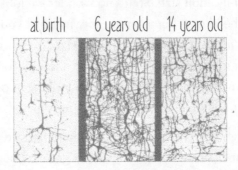

At birth, as you can see, there are not many connections between the neurons in the cortex, but as children grow and develop the neurons make more connections with each other. A newborn has fewer connections than a six-year-old, and a six-year-old has fewer connections than an eight-year-old. With each year, until the age of eight, the complexity of the cortex increases. In later childhood and early teenage years, the connections between neurons 'thin out' in a process called *cortical pruning,* which sees fewer but more highly specialised neuronal connections occurring. By maintaining only the connections it really needs and losing those it doesn't, the brain becomes more specialised and efficient.

Nevertheless, even in the most precocious of children or adolescents, there is an upper limit to their ability to do complex tasks, because the brain's design is pretty much age-dependent. As we grow, our brains shape themselves in ways that should help us think more clearly and enable us to regulate our emotions and responses.

WHAT DOES THIS MEAN FOR US AS PARENTS?

When we clash with our children over a decision we make, or a time frame we decide on, we need to remember that is not a matter of preferences by two 'equally able' individuals. Our children may be lively, interesting, curious and always surprising us, but they are simply less able to see the world in the way their parents can. Of course we don't want to limit their determination and *joie de vivre*, but there *are* times when we need to limit their behaviour, such as when they are speaking or behaving rudely, or looking like they'll do some damage — to things, to people, or to themselves.

Remember Matty Bloom. At age seven, he has discovered a new fun thing to do: ride his bike with his mates after school. The older boys in the neighbourhood often don't wear their bike helmets. Serena and Charlie are always reminding Matty to put his helmet on. If he forgets his bike goes away for a day. Matty is frustrated. The connections in his brain are not fully hooked up, so he doesn't understand why he has to put his helmet on and thinks that his parents have stopped him having fun with his friends for no good reason.

At times, children also need to be prompted about how they *should* behave, in a range of situations, until they learn the rules of the game. Until then, we are in a far better position than they are to help them become organised in mind and body. As they move towards adolescence, they'll become better at self-regulating, and they'll do this with our help, assisted by our greater capacity to see further down the road.

Overall, we can't expect our children to always understand the world in the same way we do. They cannot foresee the things that we can. While we should be respectful towards them, it's not helpful to think of them as having the mental or emotional ability of an adult. Our children are learning to navigate a world controlled by giants and, to them, it can appear disorganised and extreme.

As we will see in the next chapter, there is a limit to just how much information a human brain can take in. This limitation is almost like a physical capacity. If we are aware that children's limitations are reached far more easily than adults', we can tailor our communication with them. In this way we can help them, rather than 'crowd out' the limited ability they have to take in information. This, in turn, will equip them to self-regulate.

in essence

- Children's ability to *understand and balance their emotions* is closely related to their stage of development. As children move through the stages of development, we see gradual improvement in their ability to self-regulate.

- When children are little they're more *dependent on other people* to help them understand their feelings. As they mature they become more self-dependent.

- Children's minds gradually become more *developed*, allowing them to deal with increasing levels of complexity.

- Although children's heads are almost adult size, their brains are still forming the connections that help them understand the world.

- The *cortex* is the part of the brain that helps us make judgments, draw conclusions and assess situations, but it doesn't finish growing until we reach our mid-twenties.

- Overall, we can't expect our children to always *understand the world* in the same way we do, and there will be conflict between us.

- As parents, we are in a far better position than our children — in thinking terms — to *make decisions* about our children's well-being.

CHAPTER 3
emotional overload and its effect on children's behaviour

for what seems like an eternity, we've been taught to 'talk it out' with our children if they misbehave. I'm not exactly sure why this is the case. But if we do this every time our children's behaviour becomes difficult, many of them are going to argue — a lot — because every now and then their argumentative behaviour gets rewarded.

If the emotional temperature of a situation has been raised by the way a child feels (i.e. frustrated) or the way *we* feel (i.e. angry), then it's definitely *not* the best time to have a rational, 'teaching' conversation with them. Children who are used to escalating their behaviour are not going to be thinking straight enough to take control of their emotions. And this is a common problem in children with challenging behaviour: they suffer an emotional overload and have no way of controlling their responses.

Watch how the following situation escalates when Matty Bloom, our seven-year-old, argues with his mother, Serena, just before dinner.

Seven-year-old Matty Bloom enters the kitchen where his mother, Serena, is preparing dinner.

MATTY: Mum, I'm going next door to Joey's — back later.

SERENA: Not now, Matty, we're having dinner in five minutes. You can go after dinner.

MATTY: But I want to go *now*! He's bought this new game, and I want to see it. Why can't I go?

SERENA: Look! I told you dinner'll be ready soon. I don't *want* you to go now. You can go after dinner.

MATTY: Yeah, but I want to go *now*!

SERENA: No, *not* now ... later, Matty.

Matty gets cranky.

MATTY: You can't tell me what to do ...

Serena gets cranky.

SERENA: Yes I can — I'm your mother and I'm in charge here, *not* you.

Matty begins to lose control.

MATTY: But I promise I'll be back before dinner!

Serena gives Matty the death stare and becomes more fierce.

SERENA: Don't give me that, Matty. Last time you took off to Joey's, I had to leave the dinner cooking and come and find you. The chops got burnt and it was all your fault!

Matty completely goes off his tree.

MATTY: GET LOST, MUM! I'M GOING ANYWAY!

Serena begins to yell — big time.

SERENA: NO, YOU'RE NOT! GET BACK HERE *NOW*!

It's easy to see how Matty has developed a pattern of arguing whenever he takes a different view from his mother. In the past, whenever Serena has told Matty what she wants from him, Matty has argued. More often than not, Matty's mental accelerators have urged him to press on. His brakes may have been half-engaged, but he has always been hard-pressed to make them grip.

Serena is increasingly exhausted by Matty's behaviour. She's never been sure what to do when he does this, and now she's caught in a pattern that she knows isn't working. Whenever Matty behaves this way, Serena takes umbrage and becomes annoyed or angry. She sees her son behaving like a brat and sets out to teach him who's boss. Then she becomes the *enforcer*. At another level, she knows Matty's just a child, and senses that he doesn't know how to control his feelings, but she's just not going to let him talk to her like that!

WHAT HAPPENS WHEN EVERYTHING IS OPEN TO ARGUMENT?

As a psychologist, I used to see many parents with the same issue. They would say things like 'He just won't *listen!*' Like kangaroos caught in the headlights, they'd become baffled by their children's resistance and argued with them in the belief that arguing would teach their children who was boss. Often these harried parents would describe launching into emotionally charged tirades in an attempt to coerce their children into stopping whatever they were doing. From the parents' perspective, it looked as if they had only three alternatives: try to talk it out, yell, or try to overpower their children. Not great.

I often felt sorry for these folks because their relationships with their children were so strained. Many were frustrated that, despite their best efforts, situations regularly blew up in their face, or their attempts to solve problems drew a blank. Once their children were in the habit of arguing, thinking that *everything* was open for discussion, they regularly retaliated towards their parents when they didn't see things the same way.

Like a lot of children, they had a storehouse full of 'Why?' and 'You can't tell me what to do!' and 'No, I'm *not* going to do it!', but because they had become used to arguing, they used these resistance tactics *every* time they disagreed with their parents. They could not assess the gravity of each situation, because they had not learnt to sort between serious and non-serious behaviour. They just argued, whether they'd been told they couldn't visit a friend just before dinner or not to annoy a younger sibling. It all became jumbled, and the parents ended up treating every behaviour in the same way. To the children, it looked like everything was open for negotiation. This led to an inevitable clash of wills. To further complicate matters, every now and then arguing worked and they got what they wanted.

What these well-meaning but frustrated parents were training their children to do, in fact, was to argue *more*. There were more opportunities for conflict, and the implied message was that the best argument would win. The 'little barrister' received a bit more practice each time, and a pattern of disagreement was established. But perhaps the bigger problem was that while these children were attacking, *they were not reflecting*. This meant that they were not self-regulating and, worse still, they became embroiled in similar situations over and over. Because their ability to put the brakes on was compromised, they were not in control of their feelings. It was a vicious cycle that led to increasing stress for everyone.

UNDERSTANDING EMOTIONAL OVERLOAD

Humans have six senses for receiving information: sight, smell, hearing, touch, taste and what's called our *interoceptive sense*, which is the sense of something going on inside our bodies — such as our stomachs gurgling. These senses feed information into our brains. Let's imagine they are like a set of pipes that carry this information to where it can be processed. If the pipes are flooded with information, some of that information is lost and cannot be processed. It's not too difficult for a child's pipes (which are smaller than ours) to become overloaded if we yell, scream or talk too much.

Imagine that, when we are born, we are all given only a certain number of pipes to receive information from the outside world. These communication pipes carry a certain amount of noise, anger, shock, awe, visual information and so on. When there is too much information, or too much emotional content, the system becomes overloaded, and won't process any further information because its limit has been reached. Although this limit is about the same for everyone, generally speaking, adults can handle more incoming 'input' than children — and the younger the child, the less they can handle.

So, to carry this idea a bit further, let's say we are all born with a ten-pipe system. That means that we can let in up to ten pipes' worth of information. If we get fifteen or twenty pipes' worth of information, it's very difficult for us to take it all in. Children who have autism may have fewer pipes or smaller pipes so their ability to process information is even more limited.

EMOTIONALLY OVERLOADED CHILDREN RESPOND IN DIFFERENT WAYS

The truth is that if we nag, criticise or explode with anger to control our children, it's going to overload their pipe systems. There are four main ways that the human information processing system will react if it's overloaded:

1. First, overloaded children might try to *fight back* (as we saw in the previous section). Overloaded children will argue against the offending 'overloader' because it sometimes stops the argument or results in them getting what they want. Matty Bloom has learnt this. He knows that his dad will stop yelling at him if he yells back. He has also learnt that his mum will give in sometimes if he fights her. This feeling of wanting to fight is quite common in children who are used to arguing with their parents. If this is a child's pattern — to argue the point with you — you can expect it to continue for as long as it has a winning effect.

2 Second, a child may *leave the situation* in which they are being overloaded. In recent years, I have been amazed to hear from other professionals about the increasing tendency of children to run away when their parents are trying to discipline them. This happens with adults, too. Perhaps it is a developing trend to move away, perhaps impetuously, rather than to tolerate or learn to live with emotional discomfort. Have you ever noticed how when you have a fight with a partner or a close friend and it all gets a bit too emotionally charged, it's hard to stay in the same room with that person? Chances are we'll try to leave the situation if it gets too heated.

3 Third, children may choose to leave the scene *in their minds*. This type of 'tuning out' is called splitting, and is a common reaction in overloaded children. They may be there physically — standing right in front of us — but they'll look like a computer shutting down. Before our eyes they 'log off', screen by screen and function by function, until eventually they have completely switched off. Splitting is the mind's way of avoiding an onslaught of information; it is where people who experience too much emotion (e.g. fear, anger or abuse) go to another 'place' within themselves to cope.

4 Finally, some children simply *freeze*. We see this reaction in little children who look stiff and just stand there, usually when they are scared or overwhelmed. 'Scared stiff' is a phrase most of us would be familiar with.

So, our information systems react in predictable ways when they're overloaded. If we overload children with 'too much', one thing's for certain: they won't be able to monitor or notice feelings in themselves. They'll be so focused on us and our fierceness that they are unable to recognise what *they* are feeling. That's a big problem if our aim is to help them get better at self-regulating. Remember that children in these situations have a *cluster of feelings* they are struggling with. They need to be able to reflect on these feelings — and learn to wrestle with them — if they are to become better at self-regulation. Only then will they be able to manage strong emotions and not be overcome by them. Emotionally overloading children by coercing them or lording it over them lessens their ability to toggle and, therefore, their ability to self-regulate.

But never fear — there *is* light at the end of the argumentative kids' tunnel! In the next chapter, and in part 3, we'll look specifically at how you can change this so that every disagreement doesn't escalate into a fight-back scenario, and so that you can avoid overloading your children. For now, though, we need to understand what happens when these simple disagreements become heated.

WHAT HAPPENED DURING SERENA AND MATTY'S ARGUMENT?

At the beginning of this chapter, we saw how the struggle between Matty and his mother escalated, and how both Matty and Serena lost control. Serena, sensing that Matty was getting obstinate, let loose. Had she been able to hold back, she would have been able to help Matty control himself a little better, but as soon as she became angry Matty's 'old brain' was immediately engaged and *whoosh,* his thinking, rational self was gone. Matty stood a better chance of keeping it together much earlier in the exchange, but by the time his mother yelled at him he stood no chance. Unfortunately, what Serena did only gave him more practice at 'losing it' instead of controlling himself. What a conundrum for Serena. She couldn't let her son behave like that, but she didn't know what else to do.

One way of thinking about Matty's emotional ability — compared with that of his mother — is to think of Matty having a certain 'floor' above which he loses rational control, and below which he can be rational. His 'floor' for losing control is lower than Serena's. So let's have a closer look at the exchange between Matty and Serena and see what happened. In the extracts and illustrations below, you can see what is happening at different stages of the conversation.

1. SERENA AND MATTY ARE STILL IN CONTROL

In the first section, you'll see how things go when both Matty and his mother show some restraint, and are still in control of their feelings. They're in what I call their *cool zones*, and things haven't heated up to the point where they're unable to think clearly. As far as Matty is concerned, his request is entirely reasonable. He's heard that his mate Joey's got a really super-duper new game and he's keen to get over there so they can try it out.

At first, Serena is busy multi-tasking, keeping the kitchen humming while dealing with Matty's 'urgent' request. The conversation begins. Matty makes his opening gambit. Serena attends to the cooking, turns her head towards Matty and deals with the latest of his before-dinner's-just-about-ready requests.

MATTY: Mum, I'm going next door to Joey's — back later.

SERENA: Not now, Matty, we're having dinner in five minutes. You can go after dinner.

MATTY: But I want to go *now*! He's bought this new game and I want to see it. Why can't I go?

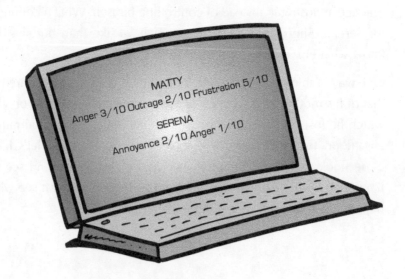

MATTY
Anger 3/10 Outrage 2/10 Frustration 5/10

SERENA
Annoyance 2/10 Anger 1/10

Serena starts off believing that Matty should simply accept her refusal to let him go next door. Then Matty, plans thwarted, quickly ups the ante.

2. MATTY'S FEELINGS ESCALATE

Now Matty's feelings become bigger, more intense and more likely to interfere with his ability to think. He has nearly reached his 'floor'; any higher and he'll no longer be thinking. He's leaving his cool zone.

'Trying it on' has worked for him before. He's grown used to letting rip, believing that even if he doesn't get what he wants, he is entitled to make his feelings known to his mum. Unconsciously, he presses down on the accelerator, not caring that he's losing his grip on his feelings.

SERENA: Look! I told you dinner'll be ready soon. I don't *want* you to go now. You can go after dinner.

MATTY: Yeah, but I want to go *now*!

SERENA: No, *not* now ... later, Matty.

Matty gets cranky.

MATTY: You can't tell me what to do ...

Serena gets cranky.

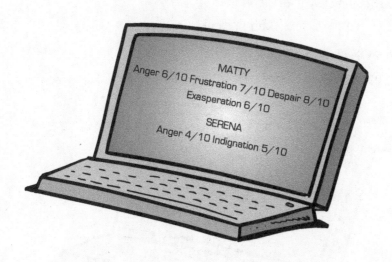

MATTY
Anger 6/10 Frustration 7/10 Despair 8/10
Exasperation 6/10

SERENA
Anger 4/10 Indignation 5/10

At first, Matty aggressively pursues his wish to go to Joey's house. In his mind, he is going whether Serena wants him to or not. As the conversation morphs into argument, the emotional temperature rises for both of them, and they are both rapidly approaching the edge of their rational zones. Serena still has *some* reasoning ability in reserve, but it won't take much more for her to tip over to irrationality. Sure enough, Matty finishes off by telling Serena his favourite 'get mad at mum' line — 'You can't tell me what to do ...' It's the final straw for Serena.

3. SERENA LOSES HER TEMPER

Matty's escalation flicks a switch in Serena's head, and she asserts her authority. Now her emotions get the better of her.

SERENA: Yes I can — I'm your mother and I'm in charge here, *not* you.

Matty begins to lose control.

MATTY: But I promise I'll be back before dinner!

Serena gives Matty the death stare and becomes more fierce.

SERENA: Don't give me that, Matty. Last time you took off to Joey's, I had to leave the dinner cooking and come and find you. The chops got burnt and it was all your fault!

Matty completely goes off his tree.

MATTY: GET LOST, MUM! I'M GOING ANYWAY!

Serena begins to yell big time.

SERENA: NO, YOU'RE NOT! GET BACK HERE *NOW!*

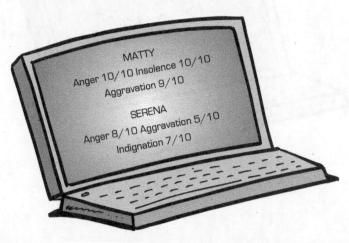

MATTY
Anger 10/10 Insolence 10/10
Aggravation 9/10

SERENA
Anger 8/10 Aggravation 5/10
Indignation 7/10

Matty and Serena have now both lost their ability to think rationally. It's a shame, really, because this pattern only increases the likelihood that Matty will apply his accelerators in the future. He'll get into the habit of blaming others for things *he* should be taking responsibility for. It's yet another 10/10 reaction to a 3/10 event. If this pattern continues throughout Matty's childhood, he'll be arguing even more than we would expect by the time he's a teenager. And that won't do anyone much good.

SO, WHAT'S THE ALTERNATIVE?

In this exchange, Matty was always going to be far less likely than Serena to limit himself. His feelings spiralled out of control not only because he's less capable of controlling them than she is, but because his mother's reaction further inflamed him. It was a lose–lose situation. That's his pattern and that's what he's used to. But it's also Serena's pattern and that's what *she's* used to. If Serena is going to help Matty behave differently, she'll need to do things differently:

1. recognise the pattern she's in

2. decide not to escalate the situation, even if Matty does

3. understand Matty's limited ability for self-regulating compared with hers

4. react in a less inflammatory way.

Otherwise, Matty won't stay 'in himself' enough to reflect on his feelings and then self-regulate.

If Serena can recognise that Matty's 'floor' for tolerating heightened emotion is lower than hers, it will have two important benefits. First, if she can see that Matty can tolerate less, she can begin to be objective about what he can and can't do. This will better enable her to see that he is just a young boy. If she remembers that Matty is only a child and is still learning how to operate his mental ability, she will be better placed to educate him to manage his feelings. She can then decide that her role is not to coerce her son, but to help him and teach him.

When Serena fully understands the differences in their relative emotional climate controls, she can choose to not react when he pushes her buttons. She doesn't need to panic; she just needs to know what to do instead of yelling back or lording it over him. Once she realises that her capacity for calm is greater than his, she can choose how to respond. As parents, we all need to recognise that we pay a price every time we let go of the leash on our own feelings — we put a big obstacle in the way of our children developing self-control, and we are more likely to need even more punishing ways of dealing with their behaviour next time.

So, this means that a *big* part of helping children manage their emotional reactions is being able to manage ourselves. Of course, you're probably thinking that this is often easier said than done — and it is. But with practice it can become second nature. We'll explore this further in parts 3 and 4, where I'll give you some tips on how to manage your own feelings as you deal with your children's behaviour.

BUT FIRST...

Before we move on to part 3, we have one more chapter — and it's a really important one. There's no point trying out new parenting strategies if we haven't identified the specific problems we're trying to solve. Remember those tempestuous kids I mentioned in chapter 1? They fought with their parents every time they disagreed, no matter what the situation, and their stressed-out parents ended up treating every behaviour in the same way, no matter how serious.

Well, in chapter 4 you'll be able to look more closely at your children's behaviour and sort it into categories, so you'll know how to react to different situations. It's not a hard process, and it will make a substantial difference to your stress levels. In fact, in the parent education courses I've run, many parents say that this simple task of sorting their children's behaviour makes a world of difference to how they respond. Many of our reactions to our children can be out of habit. By examining the kinds of behaviour our children show, we can change the way we look at them and what we do.

in essence

- A common problem for children with challenging behaviour is *emotional overload*, which results in them being unable to process what is happening.

- When children become used to *arguing every time they disagree* with their parents, it leads to a pattern of escalating conflict.

- Children who constantly argue are *not able to reflect on their feelings* because they are too busy fighting.

- Human brains can take in only a *certain amount of information* before they become overloaded, but adults can handle more input than children.

- People react to emotional overload in *four ways*: they fight back, leave the situation, tune out (splitting), or freeze.

- Keeping calm, in control and managing our responses are key to helping our children regulate their emotional reactions.

CHAPTER 4.
sorting behaviour to respond more flexibly

Anyone who runs an office will tell you that most workplaces operate better if they are ordered. If you know where to go to get things, and if the things are in the places you expect them to be, you'll be more effective. We get more work done when we can find information at a moment's notice. For our storage places to be effective, they need to be *sorted* — into folders or files, within digital systems — otherwise they're just one big mess. The main reason we sort things is so we can easily retrieve them the next time we want them. And haven't we all experienced the incredible frustration of not being able to find something when we need it quickly?

'Argh! WHERE ARE MY KEYS?'

In this chapter, we're going to look at sorting a list of our children's behaviours so that we know what to do when we notice each of them next time.

WHY SHOULD WE 'SORT' OUR CHILDREN'S BEHAVIOURS?

Every day we're likely to see a wide range of behaviour in our children. Some will be just kids-being-kids stuff. Some will be simply amusing. Some will delight us. Our reactions in these cases will usually reflect our feelings — we might be offhand, calm, appreciative or falling about in fits of laughter. However, when it comes to our children's difficult behaviour, if we rely only on our feelings to respond — especially feelings of annoyance, frustration or anger — we will probably unknowingly encourage our children to repeat their challenging behaviour.

When we manage difficult behaviour 'by feel', we end up paying too much or too little attention to the different types of behaviour. This problem of giving different behaviours the right kind of attention is an important thing to resolve. If we can draw distinctions between different types of behaviour beforehand, it will help us organise how we think about what our children are doing so we can respond effectively.

There are four main benefits to sorting our children's behaviour:

- **So we don't pay too much attention to too many behaviours.** I've seen a *lot* of parents who do this. They 'fan the flames', so to speak, constantly pulling children up on all sorts of things. This means the children get lots of attention, and respond, be it positive or negative. If we treat every behaviour with the same level of intensity, we can unintentionally reward our children for their misbehaviour. Then we're snookered. We can't let the behaviour go, but we can't *not* do something.

- **So we don't ignore behaviour that we** *should* **respond to, and end up exploding.** This is called *volcano parenting*, and it happens when parents put off … and put off … and put off doing anything about their children's misbehaviour until they are so irritated that they snap. Paying this kind of attention to children sends them the wrong message. It's like saying that sometimes their behaviour matters and other times it doesn't.

- **So we can respond consistently.** When we sort our children's behaviour, we can be more consistent. We end up with levels of types of behaviours that we have created at a calm time, rather than in the heat of an argument. Then we can respond according to what our children *are actually doing*. Sorting also allows us to identify what to focus on.

- **So we can be more flexible, less stressed parents.** By sorting behaviours, we can choose to either ignore or manage them. Not every behaviour requires us to do something about it — so we can relax a little more. Not every behaviour requires us to use the same parenting tools to manage it, either. After a while, realising that we have this kind of flexibility will result in less stress, and make our parenting roles more enjoyable.

Sorting is easy, and it is one of the most important jobs you will do. Truly.

MEANWHILE, BACK AT THE BLOOMS' ...

The Blooms have made some progress since we last saw them. They're back in Dr Wiles' office, and Dr Wiles reckons she's worked out a way to help them with Matty's behaviour problems. She has done all the routine checks. She's ruled out any childhood trauma and she's fairly sure Matty does not have autism or attention problems. His hearing is intact. She's assessed whether or not there's a physical reason for his behaviour. He's neither anxious nor depressed, and the Blooms appear to be balanced parents who are trying to set boundaries. They are also generally warm towards Matty. Dr Wiles knows that Matty is better behaved at school than at home. This is a good sign because it shows that Matty can use self-control in some situations.

Dr Wiles can see that the Blooms are good people. She knows that Serena often helps out at the school on the days she's not working, and that Charlie is a generous man who is involved in the children's sport. Dr Wiles thinks that the Blooms may be trying too hard — in fact, there's some stuff going on that that they could be less concerned about. To help them get organised, she's going to have them sit in her surgery waiting area to 'sort' their children's behaviour and get it into clearer perspective. Charlie's a little sceptical about this, but Dr Wiles assures them that they'll have a better idea about what to do if they can classify their children's behaviour.

HOW SORTING WORKS

First up, I want to make you a promise. If you get this part of Talk Less, Listen More right, I guarantee that you will cut your stress levels *in half*. This is mainly because you will be more conscious about which behaviours require a response from you, and which do not. Far from complicating your life, this simple task will help you to be more organised, and make it easier to make decisions.

Sorting involves four steps:

1. *observe* our children's different behaviours

2. *identify* what they are doing — without trying to explain it

3. *write down* what they are doing

4. *sort* what they are doing into categories

OBSERVE, IDENTIFY AND WRITE DOWN BEHAVIOURS

Observing something, then *identifying* it, means that we describe what we see, hear or notice: 'He's yelling' or 'She pinches'. These are the kinds of things we want to write down — *not* our own interpretations, like 'He's a brat' or 'She's being hard to get along with'. These statements tell us how we *feel* about what our children are doing, but do not actually *say* what they are doing. So the first step is to observe your children's behaviour, and write down what you see, being careful not to interpret it.

SORT THE BEHAVIOURS

The three main categories we'll use to sort the behaviours are:

*   ABNS (annoying but not serious). These are the ways in which your children behave that you don't consider too serious —such as fidgeting, humming or nose-picking — behaviours you're willing to overlook.

- **WANTED**. These are the things your children do that you want to see more often — such as tidying their rooms, getting dressed for school and cleaning their teeth. (We'll look at ways to encourage these behaviours in chapter 11.) These usually take some time to learn.

- **UNWANTED**. These are the more serious behaviours you would like your children to *stop* — such as hitting, throwing tantrums and answering back.

Then there's an extra but very important category:

- **BIG ROCKS**. This gives you a way of organising all the unwanted behaviours into a smaller but more meaningful list that you, and your children, can remember.

Once we have sorted these behaviours there's a corresponding parent behaviour that goes with each of them:

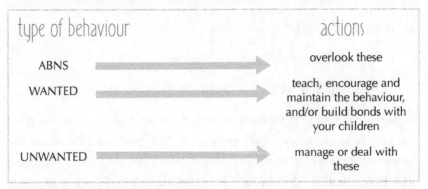

type of behaviour	actions
ABNS	overlook these
WANTED	teach, encourage and maintain the behaviour, and/or build bonds with your children
UNWANTED	manage or deal with these

Before we look at our own actions, though, we need to put all the behaviours we've written down into categories. Look at the columns in the table following. We'll use the Blooms as our example, and see what they have come up with.

ABNS (annoying but not serious)

Serena and Charlie have identified a list of things their children do that they are prepared to ignore. Not all the behaviours apply to all three children, of course it's Jessica who hums songs all the time and Tom who snorts at his parents — but they want one list to apply to the whole household. Let's see what they've written.

ABNS	WANTED	UNWANTED
Fart		
Wriggle		
Snort		
Tap fingers		
Hum songs		
Squirm		

These kinds of behaviours are ones that don't really matter to Serena and Charlie — they're small fry in the greater scheme of things. From now on, Serena and Charlie are prepared to let these things go. Serena's not sure she can let go of all of these behaviours all the time, but she's willing to give it a try.

WANTED

Serena and Charlie are clear about the behaviours they want to see more of. They'd really like all the children to be willing helpers and to pitch in, making a greater contribution to the household — particularly the boys. This is how their list looks.

ABNS	WANTED	UNWANTED
Fart	Clean room on Saturday	
Wriggle	Brush teeth each night	
Snort	Take bag to room after school	
Tap fingers		
Hum songs	Clean up toys after play	
Squirm	Put clothes on for school	
	Take dirty clothes to laundry	

The Blooms' list is getting clearer now. They know that there are some things the children do that will now be ignored, and they're clearer about what they would like to teach and encourage. Just writing these things down has already helped Serena and Charlie realise how they can change things at home. They can see that not all behaviour is a big deal, and know that they need to figure out different ways of acting to each behaviour.

UNWANTED

Now Charlie and Serena need to think about what they *won't* tolerate from any of their children. They're happy that they don't have to describe their children's behaviour in 'positive' terms, as one parenting course advised them to do — instead, they can define their children's behaviour as they actually see it or hear it. So, they fill out their list.

ABNS	WANTED	UNWANTED
Fart	Clean room on Saturday	Hit
Wriggle	Brush teeth each night	Badger
Snort		Jump on furniture
Tap fingers	Take bag to room after school	Bite
Hum songs	Clean up toys after play	Menace
Squirm		Pester
	Put clothes on for school	Shout
	Take dirty clothes to laundry	Slap
		Scratch
		Spit
		Annoy sister
		Interrupt
		Throw tantrums
		Answer back
		Bang head
		Pinch
		Argue
		Be cruel to cat
		Break toys
		Swear
		Draw on walls
		Kick
		Eat between meals
		Pull feathers from pillow
		Flick
		Snarl

Funnily enough, because the children's behaviour at home has been spinning out of control for some months, Serena and Charlie found that there were lots of behaviours they could put in the UNWANTED column — they got up to twenty-six! Dr Wiles tells them this is pretty normal, and that most parents come up with more unwanted behaviours than any other type.

CREATE A LIST OF BIG ROCKS

With so many UNWANTED behaviours in their list, it's going to be tough for the Bloom family to remember them all. So Serena and Charlie create a simpler list that groups together the behaviours they are trying to change. These are the BIG ROCKS, and sorting these out makes it easier for you to tell your children what you want from them.

BIG ROCKS are grouped behaviours — each expressed in just a few words — that describe what you want your children to stop doing using language they understand. They represent those behaviours that 'cross the line' from ABNS to UNWANTED.

Crossing the line can be fuzzy, I know — we all have a limit that's not so easily defined but that marks out the behaviour we find socially acceptable. Sometimes what you put up with at home will be different from what you'll tolerate when you're out socially. Even though you hear people like me saying we should be consistent in our approach to unwanted behaviour I recognise that where you are with your children does matter. At home you might be willing to ignore certain behaviour (ABNS) but at nanna's place it becomes UNWANTED.

As far as your list of unwanted behaviours goes generally though, you need to consider this: you can use this approach only to list behaviours you can *see*. If, for example, your child is running amok out of your sight, you'll need to approach this issue differently. This is something we'll talk about in chapter 10 in relation to holding tough conversations with children.

To create their list of BIG ROCKS, Serena and Charlie need to look over the list of UNWANTED behaviours and see which ones are alike, then sort them into a few BIG ROCK behaviours.

the first BIG ROCK

Serena and Charlie look through their long list of behaviours in the UNWANTED column. Some of these behaviours are similar. For example, if you think about it, biting, slapping, scratching and head-banging are similar — they relate to doing physical harm to yourself or to someone else. Serena and Charlie put an asterisk next to the ones they think are like this. They decide to call this BIG ROCK *hurts others/ self* because it captures the behaviours in this group, and because it is a label that all their children will understand.

ABNS	WANTED	UNWANTED	BIG ROCKS
Fart	Clean room on Saturday	**Hit***	**Hurts others/self**
Wriggle		Badger	
Snort	Brush teeth each night	Jump on furniture	
Tap fingers		**Bite***	
Hum songs	Take bag to room after school	Menace	
Squirm		Pester	
	Clean up toys after play	Shout	
		Slap*	
	Put clothes on for school	**Scratch***	
		Spit	
	Take dirty clothes to laundry	Annoy sister	
		Interrupt	
		Throw tantrums	
		Answer back	
		Bang head*	
		Pinch*	
		Argue	
		Be cruel to cat*	
		Break toys	
		Swear	
		Draw on walls	
		Kick*	
		Eat between meals*	
		Pull feathers from pillow	
		Flick*	
		Snarl	

the second BIG ROCK

Let's try to work out the next BIG ROCK. As Serena and Charlie scan their list again, they see there are more behaviours that are alike: things such as badgers, menaces, pesters and shouts. These are mostly to do with respect. But the word *respect* is a bit complicated, especially for Jessica and Matty, so perhaps *speaks/acts rudely* will be clearer. Serena and Charlie mark these behaviours with a triangle in their list.

ABNS	WANTED	UNWANTED	BIG ROCKS
Fart	Clean room on Saturday	Hit*	Hurts others/self
Wriggle		**Badger** △	**Speaks/acts rudely**
Snort	Brush teeth each night	Jump on furniture	
Tap fingers		Bite*	
Hum songs	Take bag to room after school	**Menace** △	
Squirm		**Pester** △	
	Clean up toys after play	**Shout** △	
		Slap*	
	Put clothes on for school	Scratch*	
		Spit △	
	Take dirty clothes to laundry	**Annoy sister** △	
		Interrupt △	
		Throw tantrums △	
		Answer back △	
		Bang head*	
		Pinch*	
		Argue △	
		Be cruel to cat*	
		Break toys	
		Swear △	
		Draw on walls	
		Kick*	
		Eat between meals*	
		Pull feathers from pillow	
		Flick*	
		Snarl △	

the third BIG ROCK

Behaviours such as jumping on furniture, breaking toys and pulling feathers from pillows are all to do with destroying things. A more child-friendly term might be *wrecks stuff*. Serena and Charlie know that all three of their children will understand what this means. This time they use a dot to identify these behaviours.

ABNS	WANTED	UNWANTED	BIG ROCKS
Fart	Clean room on Saturday	Hit*	Hurts others/self
Wriggle		Badger △	Speaks/acts rudely
Snort	Brush teeth each night	**Jump on furniture●**	**Wrecks stuff**
Tap fingers		Bite*	
Hum songs	Take bag to room after school	Menace △	
Squirm		Pester △	
	Clean up toys after play	Shout △	
		Slap*	
	Put clothes on for school	Scratch*	
		Spit △	
	Take dirty clothes to laundry	Annoy sister △	
		Interrupt △	
		Throw tantrums △	
		Answer back △	
		Bang head*	
		Pinch*	
		Argue △	
		Be cruel to cat*	
		Break toys●	
		Swear △	
		Draw on walls●	
		Kick*	
		Eat between meals*	
		Pull feathers from pillow●	
		Flick*	
		Snarl △	

See how Serena and Charlie have been able to sort most of the behaviours from their original UNWANTED list into just three BIG ROCKS? Now they can focus on what type of behaviour they're going to pay attention to, and *how* they'll pay that attention.

After organising her list of behaviours with Charlie, Serena reflected on how she felt:

> *At one stage there, it seemed like everything annoyed me, but when I sorted the kids' behaviour into ABNS, WANTED and UNWANTED, I could see the differences. I also felt for maybe the first time that there was stuff I could just let go of — the ABNS. There was stuff I didn't have to worry about, and I could choose not to react to it.*

A FINAL 'HEADS UP' ABOUT SORTING OUT THE BIG ROCKS

Sorting out the BIG ROCKS makes it easier to know what behaviour you're going to target, and helps you set limits in a consistent way. There are three excellent reasons for doing it:

1. **It helps you focus, and reduces complexity for your children.** The process of refining the BIG ROCKS will focus your attention on only a few behaviours you want to see less of: having just three or four areas reduces complexity for the whole family. You will have to think of only three types of behaviour, which makes a *big* difference when you're making split-second decisions.

2. **It encourages you to use the simplest language you can**, which will come in handy when you're dealing with difficult behaviour later. Language is important. *speaks/acts rudely* is a much clearer BIG ROCK than something like *being disrespectful*, and much easier for a younger child to understand. The BIG ROCKS need to make sense to everyone.

3. **It prepares you to explain to your children how the new system will work at home**. If you've sorted out your BIG ROCKS, you'll be pretty clear about how you want things to change at home. We'll look at some techniques later in the book, but before you can start you'll need to be clear with your children about how things will work. Otherwise they may be confused. Sorting out your BIG ROCKS in advance means you can prepare for this conversation.

THE BIGGEST OF THE BIG ROCKS

In my experience, the three BIG ROCKS on Serena and Charlie's list — *hurts others/self*, *speaks/acts rudely* and *wrecks stuff* — are the biggest of the BIG ROCKS around. They will probably all be on your list, too, although they may be worded a little differently. In my experience, these three account for more than ninety per cent of the misbehaviours parents complain about. I've done this exercise with more than 5,000 parents and professionals and have come up with the same results.

You may have other behaviours to add — ones that are particular problems for your family, such as a three-year-old who is biting. But these are not usually as common as the top three BIG ROCKS, so I tend to call them BIG ROCK *add-ons*. See if this rings true for you.

NOW IT'S YOUR TURN

Once you have observed and identified behaviours in your children, it's time to sort them. Write about six behaviours in your ABNS column, six in your WANTED column, and twenty or more in your UNWANTED column. From there, you'll be able to identify your BIG ROCKS. The list can be drawn up and put on the fridge so it's clear to everyone what the BIG ROCKS are and what will happen if your children 'cross the line'. We'll come back to this list later, when you might want to use it to explain to your children what will happen when you see them doing these things.

ABNS	WANTED	UNWANTED	BIG ROCKS

IT'S TIME FOR CHANGE

Later in the book — especially in chapters 6, 7, 8, 9 and 10 — I will show you some ways to deal with the BIG ROCKS. But before we get to the toolbox, we'll need to look at what happens when you move to change your children's behaviour. Changing a family system is never easy, but if you know what to expect it will help you persevere. Reducing BIG ROCK behaviour is your goal, but to do this you'll need to initiate some changes and stick to them. In the next chapter we'll talk about change, so you will have a better idea of what lies ahead.

in essence

- Sorting our children's behaviour has *four main benefits*: it stops us giving too much attention to too many behaviours; it helps us avoid paying the wrong attention to the behaviour; it helps us be more consistent in how we deal with difficult behaviour; and it allows us to be more flexible and less-stressed parents.

- To sort children's behaviour, we *observe* behaviours and write them down, *identify* what we see and hear, and then *sort* behaviour into categories.

- Behaviour can be sorted into ABNS (annoying but not serious), WANTED and UNWANTED behaviours.

- The final step of sorting behaviours is grouping the UNWANTED ones into BIG ROCKS. These focus our attention, reduce complexity, encourage us to use simple language, and prepare us for a getting-started conversation with our children.

PART 2.
change

CHAPTER 5
understanding systems and patterns in families

All around us, systems are operating. We have transport, weather, banking and health systems; a respiratory system and a circulatory system; a geological system and a solar system. Whether we know it or not, we all have a family system, too. All of these have one thing in common: they have parts that work together. That's what systems are.

If we take a 'systems focus' when we look at things, we will identify how different parts of a system relate to one another. If we can see how these parts fit together, we can figure out how they stay the same and, importantly, how to adjust them. This is an essential thing to know because if we change the way we manage our children's difficult behaviour, we will also change our family system — and we need to look closely at what this means.

One of the systems I like to talk about is a car engine. It is made up of various parts: spark plugs, fuel, battery, carburettor, leads and so on. Take out the battery and the engine won't work. Take out the carburettor and the engine won't work. Take out the spark plugs and the engine won't work. But if you take out just *one* spark plug, what will happen? Well, the engine will function differently, but it will still work. Each of the different parts of the engine relies on the other parts to make the engine work as well as it possibly can. If you tinker with one part of a car engine, it will affect other parts. That's the way systems work.

So, what's this got to do with what is happening in your family? A lot, actually!

FAMILIES OPERATE LIKE SYSTEMS

People who work with families and investigate their dynamics know that families operate like systems. The system tends to stay the same for long periods until something makes it operate differently. For example, family systems change when children turn into teenagers. As teenagers begin to forge their own identities, many families don't spend as much time together. Teenagers want to spend more time with their friends and more time on their social networking sites. This type of change in the system can be hard to get used to.

Changes to family systems can be even bigger than this. Think about the men and women who return home after being on active military service overseas, involved in conflicts in places such as Vietnam, Iraq or Afghanistan. Some servicemen and women have been greatly changed by their experiences so that when they come back to their families they relate to their family members differently. Many soldiers develop symptoms of trauma after wars, and carry the effects within them. Many are so altered that they don't know how to be their old selves anymore. When this happens, their family systems and patterns change a great deal.

What we know about children who develop behaviour problems is that their behaviour has usually developed over time. At some point it emerged and continued to build. Although all children are born with different temperaments and genes, it is also the case that family circumstances can help to form and maintain the patterns of their behaviour. Of course nobody goes out of their way to get into unnecessary wrangles with their children but if the family system tends to support children's difficult behaviour more serious problems can develop.

Don't think that I'm blaming parents. As I've said, most parents *want* to manage their children's behaviour better but don't always know what to do. Instead, by repeating the same reactions over and over, we may be supporting our children's misbehaviour without even knowing it. For example, if we routinely raise our voices at our children for misbehaving, we can establish a pattern in which they think we only mean it if we yell at them. This is not a good pattern to establish because:

- there are other, less stressful ways to get a good result
- yelling doesn't help them develop skills of self-regulation.

Remember, that's what this book is about — helping children learn to successfully wrestle with their impulses. You can do this quietly, if you know what to do.

THE BLOOMS HAVE PROBLEMS IN THEIR FAMILY SYSTEM ...

Recently, Charlie Bloom has developed a too-obvious pattern with five-year-old Jessica — he allows his 'princess' to have extra food to satisfy her sweet tooth. While Serena is really clear about this and does not let Jessica have extra sweets, Charlie, who also has a sweet tooth, regularly gives into Jessica's pestering for more dessert at the end of dinner. This has resulted in numerous skirmishes within the family — not only because the boys feel hard done by, but because Serena can see Jessica is clearly becoming overweight.

Serena, more than Charlie, is aware that Jess has been teased at school. Serena also sees that when Charlie gives into Jessica's pestering, it creates a situation in which Jessica is rewarded over and over again. She loves how Charlie is with their children — his boisterousness, his happy-go-lucky attitude and his larrikin personality — but the food thing is becoming a bit of an issue, and she'd like him to think about how he handles Jessica's 'grazing' between meals. For his part, Charlie is aware that Jessica loves him giving her sweets — it's their 'thing' — which understandably makes him feel good.

Dr Wiles sees a lot of overweight children. She decides to say what's on her mind — not just about the problems faced by overweight and obese children, but also about how important it is that Serena and Charlie are 'on the same page' in their approach at home. Dr Wiles can see that Charlie is a well-meaning dad, but both parents need to be consistent about what they are prepared to let go of, and what they are going to limit. Both have a vision of raising happy, resilient children; they know they share this vision.

Reluctantly, Charlie accepts Dr Wiles' view on the problems associated with children eating more than they need. One thing leads to another, and eventually Serena and Charlie reach consensus that, at least in principle, they need to be consistent about the children's behaviour. There'll be lots of love and special times but, equally, there'll be consistency and firmness when it counts.

Maria 'Nonna' Bartoli doesn't know it yet, but Serena's been putting off having a similar conversation with her. Serena's mother often buys copious amounts of chocolate for her grandchildren, so Serena is fighting a food war on at least three fronts — with her mother, with Charlie, and with Jessica's insatiable appetite. Serena loves her mum dearly, but she believes that the time has come for all the grown-ups to be whistling the same tune. Dr Wiles talks about the importance of all adult caregivers agreeing on matters affecting the children and Serena can see that her mother is also part of the family system.

WE NEED TO UNDERSTAND THE SYSTEMS AND PATTERNS IN OUR FAMILY

Patterns in families are generally stable. They keep repeating. If a pattern has happened 100 times, it's likely to happen 101 times. All families develop habits just by the way they live together. Some are healthy ones — such as the supportive habits of having meals together and celebrating family events. Others, such as yelling and storming off to avoid dealing with problems, are not healthy.

When paediatricians and psychologists assess children with behaviour problems, they try to find out as much as they can about family patterns surrounding the behaviour. They'll often ask parents questions such as, 'How long has he been behaving like this?' or 'When does this behaviour occur?' They'll want to know about how long the pattern has been occurring, and what maintains it. This helps them understand how the problem is being perpetuated and what parts of the system need to change to help fix the problem.

REPEATING BEHAVIOURS BECAUSE WE GET SOMETHING FROM THEM

The following illustration reflects a fairly common pattern that exists in families. As we've seen in previous chapters, Matty and Serena Bloom have developed a pattern that has been building for some years. Over time, Matty has become used to yelling to get his own way because most times — not always, but enough times to matter — his yelling makes Serena back down and give in to what he wants.

Do you think Matty is going to change the way he behaves? Probably not. Why? Because it works for him. When he yells at his mum, she often gives in. And when she does, Matty gets what he wants and Serena avoids being further upset. But every time Matty does this and Serena submits, Serena pays for it with a long-term cost — the likelihood that Matty will yell at her next time. Giving in provides her with some relief because the problem goes away, but this just makes it more likely that she'll give in to future yelling. And what does Matty learn from this? Something significant: not only is it acceptable to yell when something doesn't go his way, but that if he does *more* yelling in the future, his mother is more likely to give him what he wants.

This type of pattern, where discussions tend to morph into arguments, can happen a lot in families. It's the type of pattern that goes on and on, because the child wins often enough to make it worthwhile. In the Blooms' house, the pattern has probably happened twenty times this month in one way or another. Tomorrow, it's likely to happen for the twenty-first time, and next week for the twenty-second time, and so on … until something or someone changes it.

PATTERNS BETWEEN
PEOPLE FOLLOW
A SEQUENCE

Matty gets his own way → Mum says "Let's go" → Matty asks to bring his skateboard → Mum says "No" → Matty yells → Mum feels bad and gives in

Soon we are going to start having a look at how you can change the patterns and systems that may be maintaining children's difficult behaviour, and then in the next chapter we'll really hit the 'What to do' section. Right now, though, it's time to stop and look at what we've covered so far. And I'd like you to do an exercise. I guarantee it's not going to be hard, but it will take a little time.

REFLECTING ON *YOUR* FAMILY

I'm going to ask you to do an unusual thing — put this book down for a few days. I want you to bookmark where you're up to, stop reading and take a day or two to reflect on your family and on yourself. Watch what is happening at home and how you react to your children. Don't change anything, but *do* think about the principles we've covered so far:

- there are some trends in the field of parenting: inside-out and outside-in

- children's development goes through different stages

- children can be overloaded by too much talking or emotion

- it's important to sort behaviour so we know what to do about behaviour we see

- families are like systems and we can keep some problems recurring by what we do.

PARENT REFLECTION

Now, think about the past few days observing your family's system and patterns, and your own actions and reactions. Write down some answers to these questions.

What did you do any 'less of' in the past few days?

_____

_____

_____

_____

_____

_____

_____

_____

_____

What did you do 'more of' in the past few days?

_____

_____

_____

_____

_____

_____

_____

_____

_____

_____

ANSWERS FROM OTHER PARENTS WHO TRIED THIS EXERCISE

After doing this exercise with thousands of parents, I found similar answers reappearing time after time:

- *I talked less this week — it was hard, but I realised that I was pulling my son up for too many things. Knowing about ABNS helped me to make a decision not to nag him as much. There are bigger things to worry about than things that are just a bit annoying!*

- *I only spoke up a few times. She's really a good kid.*

- *I yelled less.*

- *I saw more ABNS than before.*

- *I was much more willing to let things go this week.*

- *The hardest part of just 'watching' was not saying anything.*

YOU *CAN* CHANGE PATTERNS IN YOUR FAMILY

There are many examples of how other people attempt to change the way we do things. In recent years we've been asked to adjust our behaviour in many ways, such as:

- using sunscreen to prevent skin cancer — slip, slop, slap

- taking reusable bags to the supermarket to save on plastic bags

- using rainwater tanks and other water-saving techniques to limit our water wastage

- using self-service check-outs at supermarkets to save on their staff costs.

It takes some time to get used to these changes. You and your children will experience something similar when your family patterns change. If your children have been misbehaving in a patterned way, they will usually have been in this pattern for some time. When you change the pattern, there will be some teething problems and your children will need some time to get used to a new way of doing things.

ADAPTING TO SYSTEM CHANGES

Here's a personal story that illustrates how we may resist change to familiar systems, and how that resistance can be overcome — with time, and with the right help.

About six years ago, I began conducting regular training programs in Australia and New Zealand. At the time, the airline I used introduced a system for processing passengers — self-check-in kiosks. These are the machines at the entrance of an airport terminal that look like ATMs, and they produce a boarding pass once you've entered your name and flight booking details.

The first time I entered a check-in queue after the kiosks were installed, a member of the airline's ground crew approached me, saying, 'Hello, sir, can I show you how to use our new self-check-in facility?' She pointed at the machine. 'Do you have your booking number?'

Because I was used to being checked-in at the service counter, I resisted the staff member's efforts to bring me into twenty-first century. Grimacing slightly, I asked, 'Is there someone I can talk to instead?' Although I wasn't rude, I was a bit put out by this development, and reluctant to play ball with the airline's efforts to 'teach' me this new way of doing things.

Each time I went to the airport after that, something similar happened: 'Sir, can I help you? May I show you how to use the self-check-in kiosk?' In the back of my mind, I was convinced this was yet another way for a corporation to get me to do its work for it. I also knew this new process would take jobs away from people. But a third part of my resistance — if I am to be truthful — was that I was not confident about using the touchscreen on the machine. It was unfamiliar, and I wasn't sure if I could do what was required.

The first few times this happened, I was not motivated to overcome my mental block. I probably appeared disengaged, listless and apathetic. My facial expressions would have been blank, my arms folded. All the outward signs would have reflected my lack of enthusiasm. On later occasions, though, when I had more time, the ground crew were more easily able to engage me. 'I'm not in a rush,' I'd think, 'so why not?' Each time the staff member's approach was the same, and each time I agreed to be engaged I learnt more, bit by bit, about what was going on.

The airline was getting me more used to what it wanted me to do. The staff reassured and coached me. Slowly but surely I was being cajoled and encouraged to change over to the new system. Eventually, the staff trained me so well that when other people from my office accompanied me to training workshops I would sometimes try to train *them* to use the self-check-in kiosks: 'Do you know how to do this? I do! Come over here and I'll help you.'

The airline's goal was to make using its self-check-in system the 'normal' way of doing things, changing the behaviour of tens of thousands of passengers in the process. The airline's management knew this was going to take time and effort. It knew that not everyone would welcome this change and the airline would have to persevere, training its staff to deal with resistant customers. The airline knew that it didn't have to achieve everything at once. It couldn't. Clearly, its staff would encounter a wide range of customers — young people, elderly people, people experienced in using touchscreens, people with no experience. Some customers had even stronger views than I did about doing corporations' work for them; others, like me, just preferred being served by real people.

CHANGING OUR FAMILY SYSTEMS TAKES TIME

When it comes to changing systems within a family, I want you to remember this: children think in the moment, but you need to think in weeks or months. Just as the airline had a long-term plan to change its customers' behaviour, you need to take a longer-term view of change than your children. And if you're going to try to change their behaviour, it's likely that the system — your family system — will struggle to adjust to this new way of doing things, at least for a while.

But you're reading this book for a reason — because you *want* to do things differently. When you see the need for change in your family, you have to face up to one important fact: the only person who is going to change a pattern in an adult–child pattern is *you*, and it could take months. You can also expect your children to be reluctant participants, simply because they have become used to things happening in a certain way. Just as adults resist change, your children are not likely to welcome your efforts to improve their behaviour.

At these times, you'll need to behave towards your children like the airline's staff behaved towards me — persistent, calm and helpful. Even if it takes time to see improvements, you shouldn't be discouraged or tempted to revert to old habits such as raising your voice or coercing your children to behave. If you're consistent, you *will* see positive changes happening. Consistency is the key.

CHILDREN WILL TEND TO RESIST CHANGE

When you attempt to change behaviour that has developed over time, your children will resist your efforts to shape their behaviour and, at times, step up their resistance in an effort to return the pattern to what it was. They, like you and I, are creatures of habit. They've probably been used to things happening a particular way for a long time so they'll resist and complain and want things to stay the way they are. This type of disruption can take various forms.

Here are a few ways that children behave if they are confronted about their behaviour. These are signs of resistance we can predict if we confront them about their behaviour but, if we persist this behaviour will lessen:

Pleading with you   **Fuming**   **Defying you**

Looking for sympathy   **Throwing a tantrum**

The main message here is that children try to *resist* change, and it's important not to take their misbehaviour personally. These behaviours are not attempts to punish you or to aggravate you but are usually spontaneous attempts to reinstate the status quo. Children getting angry at us for not doing things as they would like is not going to make them hate us. Unfortunately, though, I've seen many parents worry too much about keeping on good terms with their children. But here's the thing: your children and you share a wonderful bond called attachment, which is strong, very strong. Nearly every child forms this attachment and most form it *securely*, which basically means your relationship with them, and theirs with you, is going to withstand an 'I hate you!' or a 'You're a mean, horrible mum/dad!' when things don't go as a child would like them to.

So, trust in your attachment. It's strong and it's there. They won't end up hating you because you've set a boundary. In fact, one day, many years from now, they may thank you.

THE DAY CHANGE CAME TO MATTY BLOOM'S HOUSE

Matty Bloom is about to experience a change at home. Having seen Dr Wiles to get some clues about what to do, the Blooms are gearing up for what they will do if Matty misbehaves.

You may remember Matty's behaviour from previous chapters. Matty:

- he yells a lot

- he is often defiant

- he gets easily exasperated when things don't go his way

- he often pesters his parents

- he has a limited ability to stop himself from becoming outright defiant.

You might think that if the Blooms were doing all the 'right' things, Matty's behaviour would decrease over time. We can show this on a graph. As time progresses, his yelling behaviour would, you would think, simply become less frequent.

Reducing unwanted behaviour

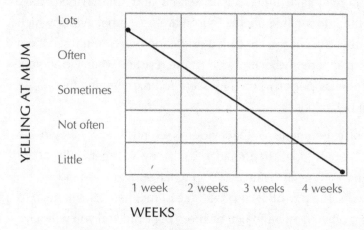

At the start of week one, Matty is yelling at his mother 'lots'. Then, as the weeks go by, the amount of yelling lessens from 'lots' to 'often' to 'sometimes' to 'not often' to 'little' over a four-week period.

But in reality a decrease in Matty's yelling is not necessarily going to be this smooth. This second graph shows how it's likely to happen.

But it would probably look more like this

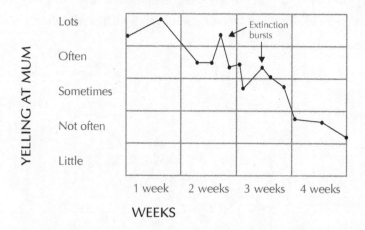

Changes in anyone's behaviour rarely go smoothly. It's not usually a straight-line thing. What will happen is that many of Matty's outbursts may, in fact, worsen before they get better. His yelling may initially increase because he wants the pattern back the way it was. Changing his behaviour will take time. But if Serena and Charlie persevere, they will settle into a new pattern. These flare-ups in behaviour which accompany times of change are called *extinction bursts*. You'll see them when children apparently become even more resistant when we attempt to limit their behaviour or when they seem to be improving then lapse into difficult behaviour.

Thousands of experiments by behavioural scientists have shown the same thing: people don't like change, but they will generally adapt with time and with perseverance by the 'change agent' — and in this case, that's you. The pay-off is also that, over time, parents will need to intervene less often, family life will be more peaceful and you will have more energy for the fun activities. And that has to be worth some initial resistance, doesn't it?

SO WHAT COMES NEXT?

In the next section, I'm going to show you some behaviour change tools that I hope will increase your choices for dealing with different sorts of behaviour. Like any DIY project, you will need different tools to complete various parts of the job. Each of the coming chapters will show you quite different parenting strategies aimed at building self-regulation in your children and fostering your relationship with them.

in essence

- Families operate like *systems*, and have parts that work together. Within these systems are many *patterns* that determine how family members behave.

- Family systems tend to *stay the same* for long periods and patterns tend to repeat until something makes them operate differently.

- Children's difficult behaviour builds up over time, and often it is the family system that helps *maintain this behaviour*. Parents do not intend this to happen.

- In the adult–child relationship, it is only the *adult* who can really change a family pattern.

- With any change to a family system or pattern comes a *struggle to adjust* to the new way of doing things, at least for a while. Making changes to anyone's behaviour rarely goes smoothly.

- Change in a family takes *time* — weeks, months or longer.

- Children may become *disruptive* when change is implemented. There are some predictable forms of resistance: throwing a tantrum, pleading with you, fuming, defying you and looking for sympathy.

PART 3.
Managing difficult behaviour
– quietly

CHAPTER 6
a quick overview of the three choices for managing difficult behaviour – quietly

My brother, David, is a volunteer firefighter. He's told me that, at times, he finds it frustrating to attend car crashes that have occurred when drivers 'get into a skid' but don't know how to get out of it:

> We teach people how to drive when conditions are good, and they learn the basics. What we don't teach them is how to handle situations when the conditions are bad and they have to use extra skills to get themselves out of trouble. I've seen so many people who get into a skid and are not able to get out of one.

When our children's behaviour becomes difficult to manage, we tend to 'get into a skid' with them more and more often. As I pointed out earlier, when I worked as a community psychologist, the vast majority of parents I saw didn't visit our centre because things were going well at home. They came because they were sick and tired of doing things that didn't work. Faced with children who wanted to argue all the time, they found it increasingly hard not to retaliate.

A USEFUL 'DROP-DOWN MENU'

So, when faced with a 'skid', how *do* we overcome those instincts and make the best decision to manage our children's behaviour? We need a simple set of principles or strategies to refer to so that we don't wind up using our feelings as the sole basis for our responses. If we have a simple, easy-to-remember model of what to do we have a better chance of responding consistently and calmly even when our moods are fluctuating or the children are just having a bad day. When everything is going haywire, this will be your anchor point so you won't be tempted to do something you'll regret later.

The three main strategies I'm going to show you will give you an easily accessible list to help you remember what to do when you get into a skid with your children. I call this tool a *thought organiser* — something that's easy to remember and that helps you work out what to do. Thought organisers can take many forms, such as getting-started guides, cheat sheets, rhymes, catchphrases, acronyms (e.g. SWOT — strengths, weaknesses, opportunities, threats) and simple visual cues. The 'three choices' model is a simple thought organiser to help you decide how to manage your children's behaviour.

WHAT IS THE 'THREE CHOICES' MODEL?

Think back to chapter 4 when you identified and sorted your children's behaviour into ABNS, WANTED and UNWANTED behaviours. I said there was a parent action that corresponded to each of these:

- ABNS: consciously overlook this type of behaviour

- WANTED: teach, encourage and/or build bonds with your children

- UNWANTED: manage or deal with the behaviour.

Later in the book we'll have a better look at how to promote WANTED behaviours (see chapter 11). But now we'll concentrate on the ABNS and UNWANTED behaviours, and this is where the three choices model comes in. It will help you work out what to do next when your children are misbehaving, and it's easy to remember.

In the three choices model, you have three options when faced with your children's difficult behaviour:

- ignore your child's behaviour (if the behaviour is annoying, but not serious)

- signal your child to stop what they are doing and attempt to shift their attention (if the behaviour is a BIG ROCK)

- emotion-coach your child (if the behaviour isn't aimed at you or if it isn't a BIG ROCK).

In the next three chapters, I'll go over these three choices in detail to describe how they work, and what you can do to use each of them.

CONSENSUS HELPS

Before we dive into the detail, though, I need to mention one more principle that will really help you use the three choices model to its best effect: consensus. If it's at all possible, *all* the adults in your family (even if they live in different homes) should be on the same page. Of course this isn't always possible all of the time, and each adult who cares for your child or children will bring their own differences and unique styles to the job. But if you can keep some really important principles consistent, it will save a lot of distress and avoid conflict that your children can see — disunity that may add extra conflict to an already challenging mix.

That's the thing with the three choices model. As much as is humanly possible all the adults need to use the model consistently and calmly.

HOW WILL CONSENSUS HELP THE BLOOMS?

The pay-off for the adults in the Blooms' house is that there is more predictability in responses. Charlie, Serena and Nonna Bartoli have all discussed the BIG ROCKS they need to manage better, and have agreed to support one another in using the three choices model. They have also discussed other specific problems, such as the dilemma of Charlie and Nonna Bartoli letting Jessica eat too many sweets (see chapter 5). This was an inconsistency in the Blooms' home, where some adults were more lax than others when it came to food. If Jessica was to change her eating habits, all three adults needed to take the same approach: some treats are OK, but not all the time. They have agreed that sweets after dinner on Saturdays are OK but not at other times. If Charlie or Nonna want to spoil Jessica or the boys, they will play a game with them, such as handball or hula hoops or football.

in essence

- When we 'get into a skid' with our children we need a *simple set of strategies* to refer to so we don't base our responses on our feelings or moods alone.

- The three choices model is a *thought organiser*, or a simple way of remembering what to do.

- If it is at all possible, all the adults in your home should reach *consensus* on the use of the model to avoid disunity, extra conflict and inconsistent messages for the children.

CHAPTER 7
ignoring behaviour – and managing yourself

back in chapter 4 when we sorted our children's behaviour, we tried to work out which behaviours were not worth reacting to. These are the ABNS and I suggested you make a list of them. The idea was to decide which behaviours you could make a conscious decision to ignore. Is your child's wriggling really that serious? Can you live with those episodes of pouting, sulking or whining? These are the kinds of questions you asked yourself.

Because really, in the broad sweep of things, some behaviour is just *not* worth paying attention to. And if you do pay attention to it when you don't need to, you risk eroding your relationship with your children and you may end up in combat over problems that will probably just sort themselves out. Have a look over your list of ABNS. You have already decided that these behaviours are not serious and not worth doing anything about. Better to let these ones go than make a big deal of them.

So, when confronted with difficult behaviour from your children I suggest you quickly ask yourself these questions:

- Is this on my list of ABNS?

- Is this behaviour just ticking me off and not worth reacting to?

- Is this something that will sort itself out in time?

- Do I need to take action here?

This will help you decide whether to ignore the behaviour or not.

Remember that an important part of parenting is knowing what behaviour to overlook. It's as much about what you *don't* do as what you do. It's not always easy, but it will help you focus on what you really *do* need to manage.

Remember, too, that *context* plays an important part in what we allow or don't allow our children to do. For example, what you tolerate at home may not be acceptable at a family barbecue. Some of us may allow our children to swear as long as they're not insulting or abusing anyone, but we wouldn't want this to happen at grandma's house. So, there are, if you like, 'public' versus 'private' contexts — places and situations where you can let things slide and others where you need to help your children take social circumstances into account.

Whatever you decide you need to figure out what you will do in certain circumstances. It's your family — *you* have to work out your BIG ROCKS — and it's a subjective thing that depends on your values and the importance you place on the views and responses of people outside your family. In any case, you'll need to be aware that, one, consistency is important for your children and, two, they may not have a full understanding of the difference between similar situations. They will need your help and guidance.

TO IGNORE BEHAVIOUR, WE NEED TO MANAGE OURSELVES FIRST

In chapter 5, when we looked at family systems, we established that when we implement any changes our children's behaviour might get worse in the short term. Any change to one part of a family system affects *every* part of the system in some way — and that includes parents. So, when your children become angry in an attempt to get the system back to the way it was, you may be tempted to retaliate, especially in the early days. But remember: you *can* overcome this habit of fighting back. I can teach you a way to do this, but the rest is up to you.

Holding 'steady as she goes' under pressure is really important so we can send our children the message that we are reliable and consistent.

PRACTISE LIMITING YOURSELF IF YOU WANT YOUR CHILDREN TO DO THE SAME

Choosing to ignore some of our children's behaviours rather than overreacting means that we have to limit ourselves first. Psychologist Daniel Goleman talks about the role of the 'observer self' in adults — the ability to observe emotions in ourselves but not be overcome by them. The ten- to thirteen-year-old boys I mentioned in chapter 1 were only *just* becoming aware that this ability even existed in them.

We notice this ability to observe feelings in our self but not be overcome by them when we experience frustration on the inside but outwardly appear composed and cool. Like a duck gliding on water, the scene on top appears calm but underneath a lot is going on. When we're able to observe and notice emotions like this but not be consumed by them, it's a sign of our maturity. Of course, holding on to our emotions becomes even more important when dealing with the BIG ROCK behaviours, and we'll look at this in more detail in the next chapters.

what can you do if your blood pressure is rising?

Of course, it's very difficult to be cool, calm and collected in the moment that your children are defiant or annoy you. I mean, you may need to get better at dealing with an urge to react and get *your* mind into the right headspace. You don't *have* to react. Sometimes you just need an escape plan to know what to do in any given moment.

If you find your children are really pushing your buttons, you have several alternatives.

1. *Get control of your body.* Breathe in and breathe out, but breathe out more. Do this ten times. Your heart will beat more slowly, and you'll be calmer. If we're a bit angry already and we take in more oxygen by taking in deep breaths, we feed our hearts with more oxygen. A trick for calming yourself down is to take in less oxygen. So when you're breathing in difficult circumstances, it's 1-2-3 in and 3-2-1-*and-a-bit*-out.

2. *Pause ... think ... then respond.* That way you won't be tempted to react. Go to your drop-down menu of options — the three choices — to manage your child's behaviour. It might be ignoring it or it might be managing the behaviour by means I will show you in the next few chapters. Usually one of these will work.

3. *Ask yourself: is this a problem I have to own?* Your child may be making a mountain out of a molehill, but it doesn't have to be *your* mountain. Try to work out if this problem belongs to you or your child.

4. *Remove yourself and seek calmness.* If you are feeling really provoked, bite your lip if you need to, grit your teeth if you need to, and walk away if you need to. Try not to use your temper to gain co-operation. That may be what you and your children are used to, but it will not teach them self-regulation.

5. *Practise meditation*: No coverage of Talk Less, Listen More would be complete unless we assumed that we *all* need calming or centring times for ourselves if we are to be more mindful parents. So, beyond these quick-to-grab measures to stop your blood pressure from rising, consider regular meditation. There is increasing research demonstrating that a small amount of mental stillness in our day can and does help us all to self-regulate more easily. See the 'mental stillness' website in the resources and further reading section.

IT WON'T WRECK YOUR RELATIONSHIP TO REMAIN DETACHED

When you are faced with your children's difficult behaviour, you'll need to remember that it's OK to change gears in a difficult parenting moment. This means that you can move from warm and emotional, to calm, and then to firm and unemotional. And it's a key skill to master when you're using any of the three choices — ignoring, signalling or emotion coaching.

This temporary aloofness or detachment is necessary to help our children develop self-regulation. We can still be warm, connected and attached most of the time, but when our children kick off some difficult behaviour, it is not business-as-usual. Different strategies apply. Instead, we need to go to that part of our minds where we can remain rational and concentrate on what needs to happen.

We can learn a thing or two from professionals in our community who do this. Paramedics, for example, learn to stay detached from the distress they observe. This means they have to put their feelings on hold while they do what needs to be done. Paramedics aren't paid to be creative; they follow set procedures within a limited scope of options. They know from their study and training, and from the experience of other people who have worked in the profession before them, that they can best ensure people's safety by doing things in a particular way and in a particular order. Even on the way to the scene of an emergency, they are preparing themselves. At a car crash site, for example, they know to park the ambulance at a safe distance, leave their emergency lights on, survey the scene for danger, secure the scene, and get to work. To manage this calmly and rationally, paramedics *overlearn procedures* during their training so that they know what to do in very stressful situations. This helps them remain in the part of their brain that *thinks*, as opposed to the part of their brain that gets *emotional*. While they may be affected emotionally by the situations they encounter, they can override their emotional reactions when they are on duty.

So, if we are not going to get emotional in the face of our children's challenging behaviour, we need to have something else to do. The training paramedics receive helps them get better at tapping into a rational, organised headspace. No wonder they regularly top surveys of the professions we trust the most — we trust them with our lives! They have trained and practised, and kept on practising, until using their skills has become second nature. It's the same in many high-pressure jobs — pilots landing planes, fire fighters confronting serious fires, doctors performing emergency surgery, and police attending the scenes of violent crimes.

So, like them, you'll need to stay as calm as you can when your children flare up, and the best way to do this is to have ways of managing different kinds of behaviour in your mind so that they're easy to recall when you need them. By doing this, you will not only be less stressed, but you'll provide your children with the right circumstances for them to choose the best way of behaving — quiet ones. Quiet parenting involves parents staying calm, not necessarily the children. If you know in advance what behaviour you'll be ignoring, and when to use the other strategies I'll show you, you'll be able to override the temptation to react emotionally, and do what needs to be done.

FOR BETTER OR WORSE, OUR FAMILY UPBRINGING AFFECTS US

While we're talking about managing our reactions to our children there's one very important thing we just can't ignore: our own upbringing. Sometimes, for better or worse, we find ourselves overreacting to the things our children do because of the way we were raised. I have a saying: 'History is not a destiny.' We *don't* have to respond to our children in the same way our parents treated us.

When I was preparing child welfare reports for the Children's Court, many of the parents I interviewed were affected by the way they were raised — and not necessarily in a good way. Many were unknowingly repeating habits from their family history. Sometimes things our children do can remind us of past traumas we may have experienced, or perhaps bring up memories of how our parents responded when we misbehaved as children.

Whatever kind of upbringing we had, though, it's important to understand the themes and patterns that affected us through our childhoods — otherwise they can come back to haunt us when we most need a calm and clear head. Children will often behave in unsettling ways. At times they'll provoke us and try to pressure us, and we will find ourselves at our limits. When we are having difficulty calming ourselves down, or we find that we're picking up on every little annoying thing our children are doing, it may be time to have a good look at what is affecting us so much — apart from our children's behaviour, of course.

Whether we like it or not, we bring a range of experiences from our childhoods to our own parenting style. The following brief 'self-interview' is worth doing, mostly because it will make you more conscious of what happened to you as a child and how you could be repeating what happened in your family. You won't get many opportunities to do this in your life and I promise that by doing it you will gain new information to help you stay more objective as a parent. I know this because I did a similar exercise myself and I learnt a lot.

Serena Bloom has filled in one of these self-interviews, at Dr Wiles' suggestion. Serena loves her mum, Maria, who was the queen of order in the lives of Serena and her siblings. In many ways, Serena's respect for her mother was unwavering as she grew up. She knows that Maria did it tough after Serena's father died, but there were aspects of her upbringing she knows weren't good. For instance, Serena's father used to lose his temper a lot. Serena has realised that she finds herself repeating some of these behaviours with her children, especially when she's tired. When you've read Serena's response, you can complete your own self-interview about your upbringing on the following page.

FAMILY OF ORIGIN SELF-INTERVIEW — SERENA BLOOM (NÉE BARTOLI)

1. How did your parents deal with challenging behaviour?

   They told me I couldn't do stuff. My father occasionally smacked us. My mother used to tell me to 'do the right thing'.

2. How were decisions made in your family about limits, freedom and acceptable/unacceptable behaviour?

   Mum and dad were pretty strict. Us kids were just expected to do as we were told, right up to when we were eighteen. I don't think we got much experience at negotiating. There were strong ideas about the 'right' and 'wrong' thing to do, so it was hard to get confidence in myself and my own decisions while I lived at home.

3. What were some of the unwritten rules in your family when you were growing up?

   Do as you're told, and there'll be no trouble.

   Try not to upset your parents.

4. What did you like/dislike about the way your parents carried out their role as parents?

   Liked: They were predictable and they were warm. They were proud of our family.

Disliked: They used to make us feel a bit guilty, and dad got mad a lot. They didn't like us doing things that other Aussie kids did.

5. What is one thing that one of your children's behaviours reminds you of what happened in your upbringing, and triggers a response from you?

My kids don't do as I ask and I feel myself getting immediately angry. Sometimes I've found myself not being able to get over my feelings of anger with my own kids when they've done something wrong. It makes me feel that I've become like my dad. I see other people much more quickly resolving their feelings, and moving on.

6. Having reflected on your experience growing up, how do you think this might influence your parenting style in the future?

I will try to… be more flexible and have more fun with my kids one-on-one than my parents had with me.

I will try not to … hold on to my feelings for so long, but acknowledge whatever the problem is and get over it more quickly. I don't want to appear angry to my kids as much.

FAMILY OF ORIGIN SELF-INTERVIEW — WORKSHEET

1. How did your parents deal with challenging behaviour?

    _____

    _____

    _____

    _____

2. How were decisions made in your family about limits, freedom and acceptable/unacceptable behaviour?

    _____

    _____

    _____

    _____

3. What were some of the unwritten rules in your family when you were growing up?

    _____

    _____

    _____

    _____

4. What did you like/dislike about the way your parents carried out their role as parents?

Liked: _____

_____

_____

Disliked: _____

_____

_____

5. What is one thing that one of your children does that reminds you of what happened in your upbringing, and triggers a response from you?

_____

_____

_____

6. Having reflected on your experience growing up, how do you think this might influence your parenting style in the future?

I will try to ... _____

_____

I will try not to ... _____

_____

WE CAN'T ALWAYS IGNORE OUR CHILDREN'S BEHAVIOUR

Now that we understand a bit about ignoring our children's annoying but not serious behaviour, and we've looked at how our own family upbringing affects how we react, it's time to work out what to do with those BIG ROCK behaviours that we really can't, and shouldn't, ignore. In the next chapter, we'll look at a way to manage these quietly and prevent these situations from escalating.

in essence

- Some of our children's behaviour is *annoying but not serious* (ABNS). This type of behaviour is not worth paying attention to.

- An important part of learning to ignore this type of behaviour is *managing ourselves.* It isn't always easy, but there are ways to remain calm and not get overly upset when our children get upset with us.

- Managing ourselves also allows us to *think clearly* when our children misbehave, and to provide a *good example of self-control* for our children.

- When our children's behaviour is difficult, we can be temporarily aloof when we need to be, without affecting the bond we have with them.

- It's important to understand the themes and patterns that affected us *in our childhoods* so we can figure out why we react in certain ways.

CHAPTER 8
signalling – a quiet way to stop children misbehaving

When children can't control their urges and impulses, it's important for someone or something outside of them to act as a reference point for what to do next. When we drive our cars, we use traffic lights as reference points for when to slow down, when to stop and when to go. Just as we use these signals to guide our actions on the road, our children can use the signals we give them to pause and catch themselves, and then modify their actions. We can help them to shift, or distract their attention away from misbehaving to some other behaviour.

In this chapter, we're going to look at a method for signalling to our children when they need to stop a particular behaviour, and redirect their attention. We'll do this via a *counting* procedure that goes something like this:

1.   'That's one.' (Hold up your index finger and wait.)

2.   'That's two.' (Hold up your index finger and the one next to it and wait.)

3.   'That's three.' (Hold up three fingers and send him or her to the bedroom.)

By doing this, you're helping your children to limit what they are doing by using your finger and voice to signify that they stop. Believe it or not, it's a simple and effective way to help children operate their mental brakes.

TIME OUT

Signalling children to stop and then redirecting their attention is an *outside-in* strategy that promotes an *inside-out* skill: it encourages children to pay attention to their ability to control or inhibit their behaviour. Do you recall what we said about the role of the pre-frontal cortex in chapter 1? It's an important part of the brain where we learn to pause and control ourselves when we're in a tricky situation. Signalling aids this process by acting as a reference point and helps children learn to self-limit.

Although it may seem to fly in the face of the 'positive parenting' movement, limiting your children does *not* mean you cannot be positive with them. We let children know our appreciation when they do something that we *want* them to do. Why, then, wouldn't we also let them know when we want them to stop doing something?

My view is this: I think every parent needs to be able to limit as well as encourage their children's behaviour. It's unrealistic to always be saying to a ten-year-old who is starting to hurt his little brother or sister, 'Please play more kindly', and expect that will do the trick. This is, I believe, one of the problems that has pervaded modern parenting culture — that we feel we are not doing the job properly if we cannot be positive with our children all the time. But there are real benefits in giving our children structure and ways to learn to cope with limits.

SIGNALLING CAN MANAGE BEHAVIOUR *AND* HELP CHILDREN LEARN TO SELF-REGULATE

The concept of sending a signal is clear: it's a verbal and visual reminder for children to stop misbehaving. But there is a second, more important, benefit: it teaches children to wrestle with an impulse to behave inappropriately, and eventually learn to self-regulate. In practical terms, this means that after you have counted, 'That's one', you should wait. So count 'That's one' then shush ... nothing ... and see if they toggle. Then count again if you need to, or apply a consequence.

Parents have told me that when their children get used to signalling, the parents may only have to gently raise a finger or lift an eyebrow to send a signal. Some parents have told me that after a while they hardly need to use signalling because their children have worked out what is unacceptable and they self-regulate. But kids are still kids. They will slip up occasionally just as adults do.

Recall what psychiatrist Daniel Siegel said about this: children develop flexibility by wrestling with their impulses. So, it's a practice thing. Brad Williams, a colleague of mine, says that signalling reminds children to tap into their 'wise-part'. If we can help them to *toggle* (see chapter 1) or reflect *before* their behaviour escalates into conflict, they stand a better chance of holding themselves in check.

SIGNALLING HELPS KEEP CHILDREN IN THEIR COOL ZONE

When we signal, we are asking our children to pull back from escalating their behaviour. We put the ball back into their court, giving them practice at choosing what they will do. By repeating this practice of pulling back from escalating, children learn to operate their mental brakes which in turn develops their mental flexibility. They learn about limits, but they also learn how to develop self-regulation. This is why pausing between counts is so important — it encourages children to stop, think and, hopefully, toggle before reacting.

REMEMBER THAT SELF-REGULATION CAN BE TAUGHT AND LEARNT

You'll remember our rugby player in chapter 1 who was switching between his old brain and his new brain. By signalling children, I believe we are strengthening this ability. We are saying, 'You need to redirect your behaviour'. It's this cue to reflect, practised many times over; that will result in the building of neural pathways that will help them use their mental brakes. Signalling helps children redirect to a thoughtful place in their minds, where they can get a grip and stop their behaviour. If they practise this skill thousands of times across their childhood their mental braking will work better. And guess what? You won't have to parent from the outside-in as much as they get older.

When we yell at our children to gain their compliance, though, they often don't learn how to redirect their attention, work their brakes and manage themselves. To be quite frank, if we just yell they get overloaded (see chapter 3) and then won't self-regulate. If they can't reflect, they can't self-regulate. It's that simple.

Of course I'm not the only person to have considered the counting method for signalling children to stop their misbehaviour. One of my mentors in the area of signalling, Dr Tom Phelan, shows how parents can warn their children to behave properly by counting, and by indicating to them that they need to stop certain behaviour. Other parenting authors and researchers have talked about similar approaches, such as Nigel Latta, Carl Pickhardt, Janet Heininger and Sharon Weiss, and Jo Frost (aka 'Supernanny'). While some of these authors have highlighted this technique as a warning to stop certain behaviour, less has been said about it as an opportunity to teach children how to *toggle* and eventually learn to self-regulate. This is really what *quiet parenting* is all about.

SOME PEOPLE HAVE CONCERNS ABOUT SIGNALLING

I've heard a few concerns from parents about the counting approach. They worry that it might be too negative, or that counting is just a way of giving a warning to children that doesn't teach them anything. Another concern is that it may suppress children's emotions. When I hear these concerns, I have three responses:

1. Remember that nobody goes through life without being limited.

2. If it is true that our ability to contain our emotions will get better only if we practise using the part of our brain that limits behaviour,

how will our children learn to contain their behaviour if they do not learn when, and how, to pull back?

3. We can limit children's misbehaviour while helping them live full emotional lives. This is something we will cover more fully in the chapter on emotion coaching.

WHAT BEHAVIOUR SHOULD WE USE COUNTING FOR?

Try to remember that the main purpose of signalling is to help children assume better self-regulation, and that it's those BIG ROCKS that you really want your children to stop. When you use signalling to stop the BIG ROCKS, what you're doing is helping them catch themselves before losing control and shifting their attention to a different response.

HOW SHOULD WE DELIVER SIGNALLING?

The signalling process needs to be delivered firmly but *not in a menacing way*. This is really important. A signal is *not* a threat — it is a way to help your children catch themselves and to get better at learning a skill you are teaching them. Here's the thing about delivery: if you are to evoke a toggling response, you'll need to make sure you say nothing between counts — *nothing*. This is their reflective space, their opportunity to make a choice.

Counting can work as:

- a *nudge* ('I want to remind you that you need to stop pushing over your brother's building.')

- a *clear signal* ('I really mean what I'm saying here, you need to stop yelling at me.')

- a *firm direction to stop* ('What you are doing — knocking over your little brother's artwork — is unacceptable.')

- a *way of interrupting conflict* ('We all need some space apart from one another, so you can go away and calm down.')

- a *reminder* about the rules in your family and the way you live together.

LET'S LOOK AT COUNTING IN PRACTICE

1 Serena and Matty arguing as usual

2. Serena tries signalling and it works

To see how the signalling works I invite you to go to the website www.michaelhawton.com or click on the QR code below. There you'll find an animation exclusively available to people who do our courses or who have purchased this book.

NOW, HERE'S HOW YOU DO IT

To start a new signalling system in your home, you'll need to do some preparation. Then it needs to be implemented clearly, calmly and consistently.

PREPARE AN EXPLANATION OF SIGNALLING

For your children to understand how the new signalling system works, you'll need to prepare them for what will happen. It's like those traffic signs on the road that tell you in advance what to expect before you get to a camera or different speed zone: '60 AHEAD, REDUCE SPEED', 'HEAVY FINES APPLY', and so on. These signs let drivers know what to do (slow down), but also indicate what will happen if they don't. It's the same with your children: you need to tell them that *they will be expected to stop* at your signal when you count, and what will happen if they decide not to.

Your explanation doesn't have to complicated, but it has to be clear. It's probably not going to be the type of conversation you will have very often with your children but by rehearsing *beforehand* you can make a *big* difference as to how it turns out.

So, the first step is to write down (or draw) *what* it is that you want your children to stop doing. This part of the task will be relatively easy if you have completed the earlier task of sorting out the BIG ROCKS. On the following page, write down the behaviours that you want your children to stop. They're the ones you'll use the counting for. It's a good sheet to put on your fridge, so it's clear to everyone what's going on. This will help you describe what you are going to say.

Big Rock behaviours

You, _____, will be 'counted'

for doing the following:

1 _____

2 _____

3 _____

When you do these things, we'll say:

'That's one'.

That's a choice, and you're supposed to stop.

If we get to 'That's three', you'll have to go to

_____

and stay there for_____ minutes.

Next, I suggest that you write out what you are going to say. This is not essential, but we all know we get much clearer about what we're going to say if we have a go at writing it first. By doing this, you'll more easily remember what to say if your child interrupts you. (There are a few ways to deal with this, but writing things down is a good start and will help you stay focused on getting the message across if your children try to side-track you.) Keep your message simple:

> *Your dad and I sometimes see you misbehaving by talking rudely or hurting other people. When you do these things in future, we are going to put our finger up and say: 'That's one.' You need to stop whatever you are doing when we do this. If you keep going, we will put two fingers up and say, 'That's two.' That's your second chance to stop. If you still keep going, we will say 'That's three' and you will have to go to your room for a break away from the rest of the family. If what you do is really bad, we'll say 'That's three' straightaway and you'll have to go to your room.*

For children under five, your descriptions need to be even simpler:

> *If mummy or daddy sees you behaving in a naughty way, we will count you: 'That's one, two, three.' You have to stop doing what you are doing when we count you. If we count to three you need to go to your chair and sit there until we say you can go and play.*

With under-fives, don't worry about getting them to tell you what they understand — just start counting and they will get it.

Then think about how you're going to have this conversation. It's best to set it up for a time when your child is likely to be alert. This is when you have the best chance of gaining co-operation; introducing a new system when children are tired or sick is not a good idea.

GET THE MESSAGE ACROSS, AND CHECK THEY UNDERSTAND

One way of having the getting-started conversation is to break it up into three steps (RTA):

- **r**eward them for listening

- **t**ell them what's going to happen

- **a**sk them what they understand by it.

So, first, *reward* them for listening:

> *Dad and I want to have a talk with you before we have dinner. What we need from you is for you to not talk for five minutes while we explain something to you. The reward for you not talking while we are talking is we will go to the park to throw your new boomerang. Do you reckon you can be quiet while we talk?*

Second, *tell* them — explain how the system will work:

> *We want to try a new idea for dealing with the things we really don't like you doing. We've been having some problems with you answering us back and hurting other people. Well, we're going to try something different.*

> *We've made a list of things we want you to stop doing. See these things here? [Point to the list you have put up on the fridge.] When we see you doing those things we're going to say, 'That's one.' That's a chance for you to stop. If you stop, we won't say anything else. But if you keep doing these things, we'll say, 'That's two.' That's your second chance to stop. If you keep going, we'll say, 'That's three' and you'll have to go to your room for [one minute for each year of the child's age] minutes. But sometimes if what you do is really awful, we may say 'That's three' and you'll go to your room straightaway.*

> *When you come out of your room, we're not going to talk about your behaviour.*

Third, *ask* your child to tell you what you just said:

> *OK, let's just check that we're all clear about what's going to happen. Can you tell me what I just said?*

[They should say something like: 'You're going to count us. When you count one, I have to stop what I'm doing.']

EXPLAINING THE NEW SYSTEM

Use your own words to describe what you will say here. You may want to expand what you wrote on the previous worksheet.

1 reward them for listening

_____

_____

_____

_____

_____

2 tell them what's going to happen

_____

_____

_____

_____

_____

_____

_____

_____

3 ask them what they understand by it

_____

_____

_____

USE SIGNALLING CONSISTENTLY AND CLEARLY

Mark Twain once said, 'To a man with a hammer everything looks like a nail.' Even when we have some success using signalling, we don't have to use it all the time. However, we do need to use it consistently. Here are some tips to help you use it in the best way you can.

- Save signalling for the BIG ROCKS. If you use it for every little thing you want your children to stop doing, it won't be effective when you really need it. Remember that there are many ABNS and you'll need to overlook these.

- Try to be consistent with how and when you use signalling; get it working at home first before using it in public. Many children will get it within a week or two, but it could take up to five or six weeks.

- If you're talking to someone when you see your child acting up you can excuse yourself from the conversation, hold your finger up and signal, 'That's one.'

- You should look calm and firm when counting but resist entering into a conversation with your children. Don't talk to them between counts. Remember, you're the coach in the gym of their minds! Your job is to help them practise putting on their brakes. Your role is to signal them, not to coerce or force them. By signalling them you're offering them a choice: to pursue the unwanted behaviour or shift their attention.

- You also need to avoid begging. The signal is meant to stand alone. You say 'That's one' and *wait* to see if they are toggling. If they are, you are succeeding. If they are not toggling and not stopping, you will need to count, 'That's two.'

- It's easy to fall into the trap of reasoning with your children when you use counting. Try to be conscious of this. Think of yourself as a set of traffic lights — they give drivers a signal to stop, to prepare to stop, and to go, but they do so silently. They don't expand on what they signal.

WHAT IS THE ROLE OF TIME-OUT IN SIGNALLING?

Signalling children to stop what they're doing and encouraging them to toggle does *not* rely on time-out. When you're using this system, the main focus is on helping your child to toggle. The real work isn't in emphasising time-out, it's in your child figuring out how to put the brakes on at your signal, even if they horse-snort and foot-stomp and complain. Nevertheless, we do need to talk about time-out because it is part of a bigger picture.

As far out as time-out goes, it has received mixed press in recent years. Some people have taken the view that time-out is somehow being awful to children. Some have said that for children who have had attachment disruptions, time-out only increases an existing trauma by separating a child from the connection they have with a carer. Other people believe that time-out should be banned. Here's what I think.

First, I don't know of any research that says time-out is detrimental to children if it is used properly. Like any parenting technique, though, it can be used badly — when parents place children in small spaces, or leave them isolated for long periods of time. Anyone with any common sense would agree that this is not a good way to use time-out. We should also be careful with children who have a history of difficult and disrupted attachments or abuse and not send them to a place by themselves. But when this is not the case I believe time-out can be used safely and effectively.

YOU CAN LOOK AT TIME-OUT IN SEVERAL WAYS

Time-out need not be seen as a punishment — that is just one way of looking at it. There's a few others ways of thinking about it.

1 time-out as an opportunity to separate one person from another

Just as boxing referees tell boxers to 'break', time-out can be a way of keeping children out of harm's way. By stopping a conversation and sending a child to time-out, you can limit the tension in a situation. This is especially true when children are having a physical fight. Sometimes it's important to separate children and send them to separate areas in the house. If this involves *you* going to your room ('reverse time-out'), it still fulfils the same purpose. Everyone gets some space.

2. time-out as a circuit breaker

Sending your child to time-out is a way of interrupting a situation and stopping it from escalating. In this case, sending a child to time-out can be seen as a way of curbing tension before you, or they, get out of control. Using time-out as a circuit breaker circumvents the need to lord it over your children and eventually yell at them or lose control.

3. time-out as a consequence

The word *consequence* can have a neutral meaning. It implies neither punishment nor praise. So a way of thinking about time-out is as something that just happens. It's an end point.

4. time-out as time-in

'Stay-with-me time' is where your child stays by your side or sits next to you for a while and you stand there saying nothing. Alternatively, you could have your child come with you to do whatever you are doing, such as hanging clothes on the line.

Remember, time-out is just *one* tool. If your children can show an ability to pull themselves back from the emotional brink by catching themselves before they lose control, you won't need to use time-out. When they toggle, they are using their mind to consciously control their behaviour. It's a win-win situation.

HERE ARE SOME FREQUENTLY ASKED QUESTIONS ABOUT TIME-OUT

how long should it be?

Use as a guide one minute for every year of a child's age. If they are five it's five minutes. If they are nine years old, nine minutes.

where can I send my child for time-out?

It can be a chair in a particular place, a bedroom, a hallway or some other room in the house. It's up to you. For younger children, it's often better if the place is somewhere you can see them. Just make sure it's a safe place.

what if my child won't go to time-out?

Offer your child an alternative to going to the time-out place, such as losing a privilege. Make sure the alternative is something fairly immediate and something you can carry through. It's not helpful to say, 'Go to your room for time-out or you can't watch television for the rest of the year.' For example, you could say, 'You go to your room for seven minutes now, or you will miss watching cartoons this afternoon. You choose.' Then you must be prepared to walk away and, later, follow through. Have a mental list of alternatives ready before this situation arises: loss of Wii for the day, taking away the phone for the afternoon, loss of pocket money for older children.

what if my child won't stay where I send them?

Initially, take the child back to the safe place with no discussion. Use a timer so they can hear when time is up. If they keep coming out, and they are under five, make them sit beside you in silence and don't given them any attention. If they are older tell them they will lose a privilege.

what should my child be doing while in time-out?

I don't think what they do or don't do is that important, as long as they stay there and are not in any danger. Think of it not so much as a punishment but as a circuit-breaker and an opportunity to calm down.

what should I do if my child wrecks the room while in time-out?

If your child is prone to this kind of behaviour, use a room or place which is safer. If your child does mess things up, don't clean up immediately. Let them deal with the consequences. After a while, clean it up together. Cleaning it up immediately just rewards them with attention for their behaviour (at least in their eyes).

what should I do at the end of time-out?

Tell your child that the time is up, or let a timer do it for you. If they don't come out immediately, tell them they can come when they're ready. *Don't discuss the misbehaviour.* It's a new beginning for both of you.

AFTER TIME-OUT, YOU DON'T HAVE TO MAKE YOUR CHILD APOLOGISE

This issue is a big enough topic for me to want to explore it by itself. Some parenting authors and commentators push the line that children should be made to apologise after they have returned from time-out and say sorry to those they may have offended. I expect that those who favour an automatic apology do so because they want to make the child more aware of the impact of their actions and to somehow ensure they won't act this way in the future.

I disagree. I believe a badly timed apology is likely to result in a child feeling shame, and won't necessarily change future behaviour. Asking children to apologise isn't in itself a problem here, the timing is.

Here's my reasoning. Picture this.

Matty Bloom is happily working on his Lego construction. His sister comes into the room and deliberately knocks it down. He pushes her away. She falls over and starts crying. Mum rushes in, sees Jessica crying and says, 'What happened?' Jess points to Matty and he is sent to time-out. After several minutes in his room do you think he's feeling sorry towards his sister?

When we become angry or upset, we experience a physical reaction that pumps adrenalin through our bodies. Our heart rate goes up and our nervous system becomes aroused, sometimes for hours after the event. It takes time to recover from this stress. If Matty is asked to apologise while he is in this (angry) state, we are sending him the message that his feelings are not important. We're saying he's wrong to feel angry. If we make him say sorry while he's still angry, there's a greater chance he will experience confusion rather than remorse.

The problem with *routinely* making children apologise is that we teach them to shelve their emotions. If we expect them to say sorry when they're still angry, it's like telling them to deny a part of themselves. Not good. It's not teaching remorse, it's causing shame. Children (and adults) need time to organise their feelings and integrate them before they can acknowledge the need for a heartfelt apology. Isn't it the case that we can take days to work our way through conflicting feelings when we have been wronged by someone or have behaved badly ourselves? Why should we expect our children to be any different?

If a request for an apology is necessary — which it sometimes is — ideally it should take place at a time when your children are calm and able to really listen. This may be hours or even a day later.

Some time after Matty has settled, Serena and Charlie can say to him, 'You remember when you pushed your sister? Well, we don't think that's OK. We don't do *that* in our family. It really hurt her. We know you felt angry because she broke your Lego building, but it's not OK to push her. I would like you to apologise to her.' This way the situation is addressed, but the teaching occurs away from the heat of the moment. In this way, children have a chance to grapple with emotions without their feelings being labelled 'wrong' or 'bad'. Like adults, children need time to process conflicting emotions. Wait until they have physically recovered before seeking an apology for their misbehaviour, if it's called for.

in essence

- *Signalling* is a tool to assist your children to stop a particular behaviour while encouraging them to hesitate, toggle, and then control themselves.

- One method of signalling is *counting*: 'That's one, that's two, that's three (then go to time-out or alternative)'. This gives children the choice to continue their behaviour, or to self-regulate and shift their attention to something else.

- By encouraging children to *toggle* (to switch between their impulsive 'old brain' and their evolved 'new brain'), we are getting them to practise using their mental brakes. This skill will improve with practice and sustain certain neuronal connections.

- Signalling should be used only for *BIG ROCK* behaviours.

- To start a new signalling system in your home, you will need to *explain* it to your children, check they have *understood* it, and then *implement* it consistently.

- Using signalling to help children toggle *does not rely on time-out*, but you need an end point. Time-out can be used to mark that point.

- Time-out does not have to be used as a *punishment*, but can be used more neutrally to stop a situation from escalating.

- Automatically asking children to *apologise* after time-out can lead to feelings of shame rather than remorse. Apologies, when they are needed, should take place when they can listen to you and apologise calmly.

CHAPTER 9
emotion coaching to teach self-regulation

Another important tool to help children learn to regulate their behaviour is emotion coaching. This is when another person listens and tunes in to what someone is feeling or experiencing. It can help diffuse negative feelings or enhance very positive ones.

Let's take it as a given that everyone whinges every now and then. Everyone needs to be allowed to have a whine, and everyone needs a place where they can let off a bit of steam. The same applies to children. Sometimes they will just want to express their views about their teacher, or their brother or sister, or your partner, or what the referee did at their soccer game. Don't we all love it when someone is on our side? Or when someone can just hear us out?

These are the times when we should probably just listen. Of course it's not going to be possible every moment of every day. It's too exhausting to be on the 'empathy channel' every moment of every day, but there is gold to be found when we really listen to our children.

Emotion-coaching children fulfils three important functions in helping them develop maturity:

1. It can be a powerful behaviour management tool to help *you* deal with the strong feelings your children might have.

2. Parents who know how to emotion-coach teach their children a language they would not otherwise learn. Eventually children learn how to use a 'feeling language' to describe their emotions.

3. It will build your bond with your children and help them feel closer and more trusting of you.

CHILDREN EXPERIENCE STRONG EMOTIONS DIFFERENTLY

Children see events differently from adults. This is not the same as two adults seeing events differently. Sure, we have varying ways of interpreting the same event, which is why some people experience road rage and some don't. But the way a child sees the world compared with the way an adult sees the world is not just a matter of comparing apples with apples. Children see things differently because they have fewer pre-frontal neurons firing. In some situations they will feel fear whereas we won't. In some situations they will not see risk, but we will. There are simply going to be times when we will have to use our more fully-developed brains to make decisions for them. It's on these occasions when emotion coaching can be used, especially when it comes to processing strong feelings.

If you can coach your children about their feelings, you can promote their ability to understand situations. We can use our *fully* developed 'new brains' to help them extend their *less* developed 'new' brains to deal with the situation they are experiencing. The younger a child is, the more reliant they are on *us* to help them integrate their strong feelings. Little children learn from us how to settle strong feelings. As we become adults we are better able to tolerate various emotions. But, for the moment, we can help them develop this ability.

ADULTS ARE ABLE TO SETTLE THEMSELVES

Let's look at Charlie Bloom to see how an adult's brain processes strong emotions. We've seen one example in chapter 1, with our rugby player managing his outrage, but here we'll look at fear. The order of the events in this story is important, and contains some clues on how emotion coaching helps settle your children's reactions to threatening or difficult events.

Charlie and Serena Bloom have managed a rare weekend away and are staying in a country hotel. At about 2am, when they're both sound asleep, a semitrailer comes past. At the same time, one of the local's dogs runs across the road. The driver swerves, hits his horn and misses the dog. The dog scurries off into the darkness, and the truck continues down the road, horn blaring.

Charlie wakes up abruptly, freaking out. His symptoms include a racing heart rate, feelings of panic and pumping adrenalin. For a moment he believes he might be in mortal danger. In an emergency, the involuntary part of his brain is ignited to act. It's a survival thing. Humans living in the jungle or on the savannah ten thousand years ago didn't have time to ask whether or not a real emergency was happening, their bodies just reacted. Even today, when we get frightened or alarmed, it happens. Our 'old brain' activates first and waits to be settled by our 'new brain'. When our new brain becomes *aware*, it 'understands' what's going on and begins to calm us down. Well, that's the way it works in adults.

So, back to Charlie in his hotel room. Serena stirs a little, but stays asleep. A few moments go by. Slowly Charlie's mind begins to orient itself. He starts to become more aware and thinks, 'What was that? ... Thought this place would be quiet! ... Bloody trucks ... I'm OK. It's alright. Gotta calm down ... ' In other words, his new brain — the part of his mind that can understand what has happened — is beginning to control his initial feelings of panic. This is how adults are able to soothe themselves. We can talk to ourselves and *reassure* ourselves that we will be OK. We self-soothe.

CHILDREN FIND IT HARDER TO SORT OUT THEIR FEELINGS

The most important thing to notice in Charlie's example is how easily our brains can be hijacked by our *initial reactions to events*. When we are scared or we want revenge or we get upset about things, we are nearly always having an initial reaction that may subside or become more reasonable if we can get some perspective on it.

Children have greater difficulty sorting through their feelings about events that occur simply because their new brain's harnessing abilities are still developing. The part of our brain that's geared up for survival *always* kicks in first, and the part that makes sense of threat *always* kicks in second. It's as simple as that.

When children see a threat — real or imagined — it's likely that their 'old brain' is reacting. They might be cranky after a bad day at school; they might feel frustrated that they missed out on a part in the school play; or they might feel betrayed by a younger sibling who has read their diary. There are all sorts of things that children get upset about. These are the kinds of situations that are not necessarily misbehaviour (they are not BIG ROCKS) but that can still contain strong emotional content. For parents, these emotional outbursts can be hard to watch without feeling as if we should stop them or shut them down. We may be tempted to ask questions or give advice or just tell our children to get over it. What they really need is for someone to listen.

HOW CHILDREN LEARN TO SELF-SOOTHE

As they grow up, children slowly work out ways to tolerate or control their feelings. All of us, though, learn the skills of identifying what's going on *inside* by getting reliable feedback from the people who take care of us. They give us information to help us describe what's going on. The people to whom we are attached form part of a safety network — not just physically but emotionally. They help us to understand that the world can be a safe place or, in some cases, a frightening place.

We *can* help our children learn the skill of self-soothing. We can help them get in touch with what they might be feeling. By doing this, we can help them develop a language that will enable them to do it for themselves, and which may well help them to integrate what they're experiencing. The way to do this is to use words and gestures to talk to them about what they might be feeling. Through our tone and our posture — facing them, listening with our whole body — we can show that we are 'with' them. By helping children in this way, we can offer them reassurance they might not otherwise receive.

Remember what Scott Peck said back in chapter 1? Not every situation requires a 9/10 response from us, and not every situation is an emergency. So, being able to help our children practise balancing their emotions is important, and it's a skill they'll learn — in the first instance — through their relationships with us. Over time, children will use these feeling words to describe experiences to themselves. In the meantime, they will depend on those around them to provide ways to understand how they are feeling. The resonance we feel when we know we are heard by others makes a very powerful contribution. Psychiatrist, Daniel Siegel, says this 'feeling felt' by others gives us a sense of who we are, particularly when we feel threatened or harassed. And this is what emotion coaching is all about. It offers children a way to integrate strong feelings. This is good because it helps them make sense of powerful emotions and they learn not to be scared of the strong feelings they may have.

CHARLIE BLOOM PUTS EMOTION-COACHING INTO PRACTICE

So, what does emotion coaching look like in the real world? Charlie Bloom's not sure. Dr Wiles talked about it to him and Serena, and said something about focusing on children's distress if they were scared or angry about something — especially when it wasn't a BIG ROCK situation. He had only been half-listening at the time but had quietly thought, 'That'll *never* work.'

Five-year-old Jessica has been having nightmares lately, and each time she wakes up screaming. If you've ever seen a child experience a nightmare, you'll know how terrifying it is for them. These moments when children unexpectedly wake up at night come in two types: night terrors that occur in the first part of the night, which children don't usually wake from and which they usually don't remember in the morning, and nightmares where children wake up still reeling from the terror. Charlie is about to face a situation where he can make a real difference by trying out some emotion coaching skills.

It's a cold winter night, and Charlie is at home looking after the children while Serena is away overnight at her sister's place. It's early in the morning, about 3am, and all the children are asleep when, out of the blue, Jessica wakes up screaming. She's having a nightmare. She's woken up from her terrifying experience, but she's still scared.

Charlie recalls the scene

Jessica was screaming the house down — crying, carrying on. I mean, I saw her like that, and I just told her to go back to bed. But she just got more hysterical.

I was shaking my head — I didn't know what to do. So I said to her, 'Why don't we read the "Munchkins" book, Jess?' She wants us to read that to her *all* the time.

But she wouldn't listen. 'You'll be OK', I said. 'Geez, Jess, it was just a dream.'

'No, Daddy, it wasn't … He's *not* gone,' she sobbed.

'Who's not gone, Jess?'

'The scary monster, he's *not* gone. He's still in my room!' She started crying even more.

'Look, darling, there's no monster there. I'll show you he's not in there. Let's go into your room and see! I'll show you he's not.'

I just wanted Jessica to stop crying. She was going crazy and was going to wake the boys up.

I realised I couldn't make it better for her by proving it was safe for her to go back to her room. And *she* didn't know or care that she would wake the boys. She was in such a state! I couldn't make her see reason. Nothing I said made any difference.

But then … bingo! Something that Dr Wiles had said popped into my head. That 'emotion coaching' stuff, about talking with the kids about their feelings. I worked it out. I couldn't say anything that would reassure her about the monster going away. I worked out she was scared, and that's where I needed to be — *with* her. With what she was feeling. So I tried something new.

HERE'S WHAT HAPPENED NEXT

CHARLIE: You're scared that the monster might still be there.

JESSICA: The monster's angry, and he's growling at me.

CHARLIE: I can see he made you frightened. He's really scary.

JESSICA: He's on top of the house! He's not going away, Daddy …

CHARLIE: So he told you he's not going away.

JESSICA: He's mad with me. I won't give him Berta [*her doll*]. He's not having Berta.

CHARLIE: You're worried he might take Berta. I can see why you didn't want to give Berta to him. He's so scary. Why would you want to give him Berta? No way.

JESSICA: He wasn't going to get Berta, Daddy.

CHARLIE: I can see that, darling. You wanted to protect Berta from him. There was no way he was getting Berta — no way!

Charlie could see that Jessica was becoming more settled as they talked about her fear. Of course there was no monster, but in Jessica's mind there was. Charlie wasn't lying to her; he was merely reflecting what Jessica 'thought' was there. He listened to her feelings. She calmed down. Soon he was able to soothe her enough to lead her back into her bedroom and back to sleep.

Afterwards, Charlie thought to himself that he'd done a good job of helping Jessica settle. He had managed a tough situation with one of his children by himself, and had done it by paying attention to what she was feeling. He thought a bit guiltily about how he'd only half-listened when Dr Wiles had talked about emotion coaching, and realised there *was* a lot to learn about children's behaviour. He'd handled a difficult situation that could have resulted in the boys waking up. And he knew that he'd said some things that had tuned in to Jessica's feelings. In the future, Jessica would be better able to identify her feelings because her father had helped her to recognise them.

Having been banned by Serena from giving sweets to Jessica, Charlie also realises that some important bonding has happened between him and Jessica, and that this kind of bonding might work better than extra desserts. He now has more confidence because he helped Jess to settle and go back to sleep. He knows he was there for her.

HOW DID CHARLIE DO THIS?

In emotion coaching it's important *not to ask questions*. While I suppose it's normal to want to check out our guesses by asking questions about the problem, doing this stops the flow of information. If I have a bucketload of feelings about something, and you ask me if I am feeling mad, I have to go inside myself to check in with what I'm experiencing. But if you make a *comment*, something like: 'I can see that you are looking pretty angry about this', I can answer that immediately with, 'Yeah, I am, I'm really mad at him for doing that.' I can answer you without having to check in to see if this is what I feel.

The other thing about asking questions is that children may not have the vocabulary to answer you. When we ask children how they are feeling, it's not that surprising that they'll often answer with 'I don't know', 'good' or 'bad' depending on what's happening. It's better to take a guess at what they might be feeling. It can be hard to cross the divide between wanting to ask about what your child may be feeling and trying to *name* the feeling. When I first learnt about this skill and tried to do this — reflect on what someone may be feeling — I felt like I sounded bumptious, offensively self-assured about what I saw. It sounded like I wasn't being genuine. It took me a while but gradually it became easier to reflect on what someone else might be feeling.

The main idea of this sort of *reflective listening* is to capture, from our adult perspective, what our children may be experiencing. Listening to what they are feeling doesn't mean that we agree with them; it just acknowledges *their* experience. Sometimes this is enough for them to work it out for themselves.

IT DOESN'T TAKE MUCH TO HELP CHILDREN SETTLE

Let's have a look at what Charlie did in a bit more detail. The first thing I want you to notice is that it didn't take *that much* for Charlie to get some good results with Jessica:

- changing his orientation and not trying to reason with her

- trying to be 'in the moment' with her

- using four or five key statements to lessen Jessica's distress.

I want you to remember this last point because it's important. Charlie used only four or five key statements to change what Jessica was experiencing. It only took this many well-placed statements to calm her. Four or five — that's all! And this is not uncommon. When you use this skill, you probably won't have to say more than four or five attuned statements to get a result.

Before he knew about emotion coaching, Charlie was not as equipped to 'stay' in the moment with his children. He was tempted to tell them to 'get over it' or to problem-solve with them when they were in the grip of a strong emotional outburst. Now he knows he can overcome this habit and help his children wrestle with their strong feelings at appropriate times.

Ever thought you'd like to be able to do this sort of thing for your children when they're beside themselves with rage or frustration? Well, you can. Look at what Charlie did. To help Jessica settle, all he did was pay attention to her feelings. It was a conscious move on his part. As we saw, he was tempted to tell Jessica to just get over it, or to stop fussing. But he worked out that if he just went with what Jessica was experiencing he would help her get traction with her feelings. This meant no problem-solving, no saying 'Let's get this worked out'. He just listened to her fear and anguish for as long it took to get to a natural pause.

By stating what he thought she might be feeling, he helped her connect her old brain with her new brain. He made some statements to further de-escalate the stress she was feeling:

- 'You're scared that the monster might still be there.'

- 'I can see he made you frightened. He's really scary.'

- 'So he told you he's not going away.'

- 'You're worried he might take Berta. I can see why you didn't want to give Berta to him. He's so scary. Why would you want to give him Berta? No way.'

- 'I can see that, darling. You wanted to protect Berta from him. There was no way he was getting Berta — no way!'

WHAT CHARLIE MAY HAVE BEEN TEMPTED TO DO

When our children get upset about something, we can be tempted to:

- *ask questions*: 'Are you sad?', 'Did that make you unhappy?'

- *give advice*: 'Well, when that that happened to me once when I ...'

- *dismiss their feelings*: 'Oh, don't worry about that!'

But these may all escalate your child's emotion instead of calming it. Let's see how.

ask questions

He could have said ...   ... and this is how it would have ended

'Are you sad? Did the monster make you upset?'

This worked better ...   ... and this is how it would have ended

'You're scared that the monster might still be there.'

Jessica is still concerned, but much less anxious.

give advice

He could have said ...

'You don't need to worry.'

... and this is how it would have ended

Jessica becomes more upset.

This worked better ...

You're worried he might take Berta. I can see why you didn't want to give Berta to him. He's so scary. Why would you want to give him Berta? No way.'

... and this is how it would have ended

Jessica is much less anxious as she hears and agrees with her father.

dismiss their feelings

He could have said ...

'Jessica, go back to bed. There's no monster!'

... and this is how it would have ended

Jessica becomes more distressed and struggles with her father.

This worked better ...

'I can see that, darling ... There was no way he was getting Berta — no way!'

... and this is how it would have ended

Jessica is much calmer now.

IMAGINING WHAT A CHILD IS EXPERIENCING IS A FIRST STEP IN EMOTION-COACHING

Imagining what a child may be experiencing is one of the biggest steps in emotion coaching. One way of thinking about what any child might be experiencing is to think of feelings occurring in *clusters*. I call these *affect clusters*. An affect cluster is a collection of feelings someone might be having in reaction to an event. In any situation, people often experience many feelings at once. We can picture this by thinking about the faces of a diamond — known as facets — where each face is a feeling related to the same event.

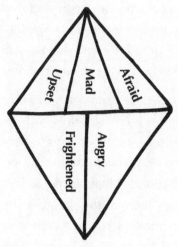

Most children will respond well if their parents reflect their feelings. In Jessica's case, she was scared, frightened, worried, mad at the monster and determined not to give Berta up. Charlie made statements based on his best guesses about the feelings Jessica might be experiencing. He picked words to match her feelings that she would understand. This allowed her to make the connection I talked about before — between what she was feeling and Charlie's words describing those feelings. Charlie's reflections were not fake. They were real, and they gave Jessica the feeling that he understood her. Charlie's tone, his attention and his language combined to show he was trying to be there in the moment, right beside Jessica in what she was feeling. And it worked.

IT'S IMPORTANT TO FIND WORDS TO DESCRIBE WHAT YOUR CHILDREN ARE FEELING

If you want to help your children by emotion coaching them, you'll need to find words to describe what they might be feeling. Remember that getting started involves making statements, expressed as guesses, about what your children might be experiencing. Yes, they *will* be guesses, and it's OK to make them. Nobody can really understand or be certain about what someone else is feeling, but if your guess is wrong, they will tell you: 'No, I'm not *annoyed*. I'm really, really *angry!*'

As well as being useful for negative feelings — anger, frustration and sadness — emotion coaching can be as useful to your children when they're experiencing positive feelings. Being able to tune-in when they are happy, excited or proud not only helps them 'feel good' but also gives them a vehicle to process positive emotion.

To help you make reflective comments to your children about their feelings, you can connect feeling words with *stem statements*. These are phrases that give you a variety of ways to begin what you are going to say. They're a good way to get started with emotion coaching, and although they might sound a little stilted at first, with some practice you'll be able to adapt them to the situation your child is facing and they'll sound more natural. Here's one stem statement you can attach any number of feelings to:

I can see you're ...   [upset]

                                        [mad]

                                        [afraid]

                                        [frightened]

                                        [angry]

There's lots more of them, too:

I can see he made you ...   [frightened]   because he's
                                                            really scary.

If that happened to me, I'd feel ...   [betrayed]

I can only imagine that you are feeling ... [mad]   about this.

You look	[amazed]	by what's just happened.
I hear your ...	[joy]	that's great!
So, it's actually that you're feeling ...	[pretty proud]	about what you have achieved.
I think you look quite ...	[excited]	at the moment.
I'm guessing that you're feeling ...	[upset]	about the whole thing.
It seems as if you are ...	[really annoyed]	that he did that. If somebody did that to me, I'd feel ... [disappointed] It's not OK to say that.
You seem ...	[thrilled]	that it happened.
I reckon I'd feel ...	[crazy mad]	if that happened to me.

MORE EXAMPLES OF HOW EMOTION-COACHING WORKS

Now we're going to look at two more scenarios that the Blooms faced recently — one with Tom's anger, and another with Matty's exuberance following a win at his swimming carnival. Remember that it's important to help children understand their positive feelings as well.

SITUATION 1 — TOM BLOOM

There's been a big fight between Tom and Jessica. Jessica is hurt and crying because Tom hit her, hard, for taking his iPhone from his room. Tom is mad, and feels justified (and still angry) because Jessica ended up deleting some of his downloads. Charlie sent Tom straight to time-out. When his time is up, Tom reappears from his room. His father is in the lounge room reading the paper.

What are Tom's feelings? Just by knowing what has happened and by looking at him, what do you think he is feeling? Here are some ideas:

1   pretty angry

2   cranky

3   furious

4   mad

5   frustrated.

These are some comments Charlie made to Tom to help him reflect on how he was feeling towards his sister. We can put the words from the list above into some sentences.

Seems to me like you're feeling …	**pretty angry**	with her, mate.
I'd be …	**cranky**	if someone did that to me.
Looking at you, I can tell you are …	**furious**	with your sister.
I can tell you're feeling …	**mad**	at your sister.
So, you're …	**frustrated**	that she keeps going into your room.

Let's see what happened …

I'll use **bold text** to show the feelings statements.

Tom comes out of his room, fuming, after he's been to time-out for hitting his sister.

TOM: She's such a little brat. It took *heaps* of time to download that stuff — *such* a long time.

Charlie sees that Tom is mad and doesn't think his feelings are unreasonable.

CHARLIE: Seems to me like you're feeling **pretty angry** with her, mate.

TOM: [*Still really angry that he's lost his music*] Well, she shouldn't've done it! She's always going to my room and interfering with my stuff. I've told her heaps of times not to go in there.

CHARLIE: I'd be **cranky** if someone did that to me. I know it took you ages to download all that stuff.

TOM: She's such a spoilt brat; I hate her.

CHARLIE: [*Thinking Tom has nearly run out of steam*] Yep, looking at you, I can tell you are **furious** with your sister.

TOM: [*Still angry, but by now he's toggling*] I'm *so* angry with her. I *hate* her.

CHARLIE: You're **frustrated** that she keeps going into your room. I get that, mate, I do.

Charlie uses just a few comments here to focus on what Tom may be feeling. He has listened to Tom and heard about his experience. Tom has already been sent to time-out for the BIG ROCK behaviour — hitting his sister — but I want you to consider his anger as *not* necessarily an episode of misbehaviour. Tom is probably entitled to be very frustrated with his sister, especially if Jessica knows she is not allowed to take Tom's phone without asking. Charlie does a great job helping Tom identify his feelings. One might expect that, in years to come, Tom will learn to express his feelings in this way for himself, instead of lashing out at his sister.

By connecting with Tom in this way, Charlie gives Tom an opportunity to express some pretty wicked thoughts about his sister. Tom, despite his anger, probably feels his dad is at least 'with him' in that moment. At no point did Charlie approve of Tom's behaviour towards Jessica. All he did was help Tom locate the words to describe how he felt and Tom started to settle down.

Charlie did a great job at staying with Tom's feelings. He could have succumbed to the temptations of shutting Tom down or telling him to 'grow up', but instead he helped Tom to process his feelings towards a natural end. Tom felt heard even though his behaviour was unacceptable — which Charlie later told him. Tom was soothed by his father's listening skills.

See how emotion coaching is a way of managing children's behaviour by appropriately confirming their feelings — not their actions?

SITUATION 2 — MATTY BLOOM

Matty has had a great day at his swimming carnival — two second places and a first place. He is brimming with pride, and feeling pretty good about what's happened and all the training he's done. What are Matty's feelings? What would you guess he is feeling — just from hearing what has happened? What do you think he is experiencing?

1 _____

2 _____

3 _____

4 _____

5 _____

Now, link up each of these feelings up to the following stem statements:

You seem …	[	]	with what happened today.
To me, you look …	[	]	
It's something that looks like it left you feeling …	[	]	for the effort you put in.

Then, if you need to, add a couple more:

Looking at you, I can tell you are …   [   ]   with your day
                                                                today.

So is seems like you're …   [   ]   that you went
                                                                so well in your
                                                                race.

let's go live again

Here's how the conversation goes between Matty and Serena later that afternoon. I'll use my words to fill in the gaps.

Matty and Serena are in the lounge room. Matty has a huge smile on his face.

MATTY: Oh, Mum! How about that win today! It was *so* great to beat Max Benfield. I knew I could do it — just had to stay focused.

SERENA: You seem **pretty happy** with what happened today, mate.

MATTY: It was so good — so *good*. Just fantastic. Really! Whoa.

SERENA: To me, you look **satisfied**. It looks like you getting up early all those times this year paid off. I'm really glad for you.

MATTY: Yeah, Mum. I know I went off at you for having to go to training all those times. Some days it was so cold, getting up that early. But now I did this, it's just so great.

SERENA: It's something that looks like it left you feeling **really rewarded** for the effort you put in.

MATTY: Yeah, yeah … excellent!

What Serena does here is give Matty's feelings some recognition. Matty put in a lot of effort — getting up early and going to training consistently — to get a result, so Serena's reflections on how Matty felt really helped him feel the joy he was experiencing. Again, all it took was a few comments that matched up with what Matty was experiencing. Serena was able to let Matty express his pride at having put in a big effort.

ONCE YOU HAVE HEARD YOUR CHILDREN'S FEELINGS, IT'S IMPORTANT TO PROBLEM-SOLVE

Over the last few pages, I've emphasised that it's important to stay focused on children's feelings so they begin to organise their feelings with your assistance if they are cross. This process should result in them toggling. To get to this point you need to 'drain' the emotion. By using your 'feeling' words, you will help soothe their initial raw feelings.

But, there are times when emotion coaching also involves you inviting your children to solve a problem, where this is possible. While it's important to help children identify how they are feeling, it's also important that they be encouraged to use their emotions as a learning opportunity or a way to solve a problem. We do this with other adult friends, so why not with our children? For instance:

- 'I get it that you feel angry by what happened. That's no good. I'm wondering if you have any ideas, should that situation arise again, what you might do?'

- 'Sounds like what your manager did seemed a bit unfair to you. Is there a way that you could bring it up with her, so it doesn't happen again?

Helping children to problem-solve will give them an important piece of the jigsaw puzzle — not only how to wrestle with their feelings, but how to think of solutions to the problems they face.

CHARLIE PROBLEM-SOLVES WITH TOM

Earlier, in Tom Bloom's case, his feelings of resentment and frustration towards his sister were very real. As it turned out, Charlie was able to help him express those feelings. Charlie didn't agree with Tom's behaviour, but he *went* with Tom's feelings. While Tom is entitled to feel angry at his sister for taking his iPhone from his room, he is *not* entitled to hit her. He needs to find less violent ways to resolve his feelings, and Charlie can help him to do that.

So, for Charlie, the next step in the process is to help Tom get his head around a better way to deal with his feelings. Once Charlie has helped Tom express his feelings, he needs to go back to Tom — maybe later that day — to help him sort out a more appropriate way to deal with similar problems in the future. Here's how the conversation could go ...

Charlie and Tom are sitting in the lounge room.

CHARLIE: Tom, I get it that what your sister did earlier today was not OK. I know Mum has talked with Jess about what she did and we will continue to tell Jess that she's not to go into your bedroom. But I also don't think what you did was something that was OK. We don't hit each other in this family.

TOM: Yeah, but she wiped my downloads, Dad!

CHARLIE: I get it, Tom. I really do. You got mad because she wiped stuff off that will be hard to replace. But I want to talk with you about how you — as a young man now — can't go around hitting your sister. I want to come up with some different ways to handle the situation should this happen again. So, let's see what we can come up with ...

comment

What Charlie does here is make sure that Tom's behaviour does not go unnoticed. He can see that Tom is justified in feeling frustrated, but he doesn't want Tom to get the message that his behaviour is OK. It isn't.

So, he brings up this topic with Tom — away from the strong emotion Tom initially felt — to problem-solve with him. If, in a calmer moment, Tom can work out a better alternative to hitting his sister, he will at least have *consciously* gone over alternative behaviours — asking his parents to better manage Jess or tell her how angry he is — rather than resorting to being violent. Charlie wants Tom to self-regulate on occasions like this in the future.

BOTH ADULTS AND CHILDREN HAVE STRONG EMOTIONAL REACTIONS

When Charlie was woken up in the middle of the night in the country hotel, he was able to work out how to settle himself by figuring out where he was and what had just happened. He *told* himself to settle down. A similar thing happened for Jessica in her nightmare. Both were scared. Both experienced their heart racing, and both were disoriented. But in Jess's case, Charlie used his calming ability to offer Jessica comfort. In both examples, their 'old brain' lights and sirens had gone off but, in Jess's case, Charlie used his more functioning 'new brain' to help soothe his daughter's fear.

Neither situation represented an emergency, but the initial strong feelings were the same. This is why it's important to understand how strong feelings often come before our thoughts, so we can use *our* more developed 'new brains' to soothe our children's minds — not necessarily when they are misbehaving, but in lots of other emotional situations.

EMOTION-COACHING WILL HELP YOU RESOLVE BIGGER ISSUES

Knowing the basics of emotion coaching is good preparation for solving bigger issues, especially with children aged ten and up, and younger teenagers. Being able to actually 'hear' how children are feeling while you negotiate will help them to integrate their feelings, especially when those feelings are running hot. In the next chapter, we'll cover how to hold conversations where you want to resolve a problem that keeps repeating and that requires a little more diplomacy to solve.

in essence

- There are three purposes to *emotion coaching*: it gives children a 'feeling' language they can use for themselves; it can be used to manage behaviour; and it can strengthen your bond with your children.

- Emotion coaching can be used when children experience *strong feelings* and need help to settle. This kind of behaviour is not necessarily misbehaviour.

- Children *perceive events* differently from adults. They feel fear and threat in situations where you may not.

- Adults are able to *soothe themselves*, but children find it more difficult to sort out their feelings. We need to help them identify their feelings.

- Emotion coaching is easier to do if you make *statements* (using reflective listening) instead of asking questions. Children often don't have the vocabulary to express their feelings clearly, so they need our help.

- A final ingredient of emotion coaching is helping children to *problem-solve* so they can learn from their experience.

THE MEAL DEAL: USING A COMBINATION OF EMOTION-COACHING AND SIGNALLING

At times it's important to recognise children's emotions to help them feel acknowledged. Sometimes, though, when we say 'That's enough — you need to stop what you're doing' by signalling, we may also find it useful to acknowledge our children's feelings at the same time.

In a similar vein, this kind of acknowledgment can be used as part of the signalling strategy. Rather than just a straight, 'That's *one* ... that's *two* ... that's *three*', you can acknowledge how your child might be feeling even though you need to manage their misbehaviour: 'I know you are frustrated, but it's *not* OK to push your sister. Now that's *one*.' There will be many occasions when you can diffuse a child's heated reaction with an acknowledgment of their emotion followed by a 'That's *one*' to indicate that the behaviour they're exhibiting is not acceptable. If a situation is escalating, and is possibly being directed towards you, you may find this strategy helpful.

PART 4.
promoting the behaviour you want to see

CHAPTER 10
resolving poor attitudes and behaviour in older children

If I've given you the impression that you shouldn't hold conversations with your children when things are out of order, that's not been my intention. There's a time and a place for holding discussions with your children — particularly when they are older than ten — about the changes you want to see in their behaviour. We're talking here about the kinds of changes that won't come about by the odd positive comment or the occasional withdrawal of privileges. These are the behaviours that need a more considered strategy.

We have focused on three main ways to handle difficult behaviour: ignore; signal; and emotion-coach children when their feelings are aroused. But the reality is that there will be some occasions when you'll need to hold a conversation with your (older) children about 'big-ticket' items. These may be problems you've been ignoring for a while but have now decided you'd better do something about before they get further out of control.

Here are some examples of what I mean:

- **Your ten-year-old daughter appears to be getting angry a lot.** She seems to be using her anger to menace her younger sister. You want to see less of this behaviour and help her resolve her frustrations with her sister in a better way.

- **Your ten-year-old son is spending lots of time wandering the streets with a group of older teens.** You know he is highly influenced by them. You've heard that some of these teens have been in trouble for stealing. You want to protect him from unnecessary risks and you want him to be safer in the company of children his own age.

- **Your eleven-year-old son has been caught stealing money from a neighbour's house.** The neighbours tell you that other money had previously gone missing but this time they caught your son red-handed, closing up the neighbour's purse after shoving fifty dollars in his pocket. You want your boy to behave ethically and to understand the importance of being honest.

- **Your twelve-year-old daughter seems to spend half her day on Facebook.** Her life seems out of balance to you. She tells you that her 'friends' on Facebook are bitches and she tells you she's going to 'get back' at a girl at school. She thinks it's OK to make threats online. You want her to return to a more balanced life and use the internet properly.

- **Your twelve-year-old son has been irritable and short-tempered with everyone at home.** Lately you've heard him talking to his friends late at night, and you've found him playing a massive multiplayer game at 2am on a school night when you thought he was asleep. You don't mind him playing games, but not at the expense of his sleep or everyone else's peace at home.

It's important to notice some key elements these problems have in common:

- Most of them have *built up over time*. They're not one-offs — such as when your child has an out-of-the-blue fistfight with a friend — but are issues that have slowly become worse.

- Problems like these nearly always get *bigger*, not smaller.

- They usually won't *go away by themselves* and children won't 'grow out of them'.

- You *can deal with these types of problems* without the conversation turning into World War III.

WHAT DO THE EXPERTS SAY?

Professional mediators, who help people resolve their conflicts every day, have invented a variety of practical steps to help them manage difficult interpersonal situations. They use *conversation rules* that allow people to negotiate tough conversations. In this chapter I will show you a template — based on the ones used by experts in mediation — that will help you hold conversations with your children about the types of problems listed above. It's called holding a *scripted conversation*.

Scripted conversations are a way of approaching difficult issues that give you a firm structure to hold on to so you don't lose your way. If you get interrupted, or if your children get upset with what you're saying halfway through, the scripted conversation approach stops you from getting startled and losing your place. Using one of the problems at the beginning of this chapter, I'll show you how to hold a conversation with your (older) children, keeping in mind the goal of *solving* the problem.

The scripted conversation method I've come up with is called PASTA.

PASTA CONVERSATIONS

PASTA stands for prepare, appointment, say, tame the tiger and agree. The idea of PASTA is to give you a method for holding a tough conversation that you can manage — without it spinning out of control.

PASTA for older children

Prepare; start thinking about the 'WHAT'.

Arrange an **a**ppointment.

Say things: something comforting, 'what' the problem is and what you want.

Tame the tiger along the way.

Agree about some things.

It's completely understandable that many of us tend to avoid having tough conversations with our children — or anyone for that matter —

because these are seldom pleasant occasions. However, if you know how to do this, you will get better at resolving problems with your children. Just as paramedics follow a process to do their jobs, you can also follow a problem-solving process that will, most times, be successful. Each of the steps in PASTA involves some preparation but after a while, you won't have to do the preparation worksheets (at the end of the chapter) at all.

To see how it works, let's use PASTA to solve one of the problems we mentioned at the beginning of the chapter.

THE BLOOMS PUT PASTA INTO PRACTICE

Your twelve-year-old son has been irritable and short-tempered with everyone at home. Lately you've heard him talking to his friends late at night, and you've found him playing a massive multiplayer game at 2am on a school night when you thought he was asleep. You don't mind him playing games, but not at the expense of his sleep or everyone else's peace at home.

Yes, this example is all about Tom Bloom.

You'll recall that Tom is the Blooms' eldest child. He's a nice kid and pretty typical of a boy his age, but his parents have become a bit concerned about some habits he's developing. They're aware that Tom has been engrossed with his new iPhone. He's been taking his phone to bed and using it to text his friends and check his Facebook. Then there are the multiplayer games. Serena and Charlie don't mind Tom playing games, but not in the middle of the night. He's not getting enough sleep (see box, below), and it's affecting everyone. It's time to have a PASTA conversation with Tom.

AUSTRALIAN CENTRE FOR EDUCATION IN SLEEP™

how much sleep do we need?

- Babies under 1: 14-18 hours throughout the day and night
- Toddlers: 12-14 hours per 24 hour period
- Primary school: 10-12 hours per day
- High school: 9-11 hours per day
- Adults: 7-9 hours per day

http://www.sleepeducation.net.au/sleep%20facts.php

After talking to Dr Wiles, the Blooms know they will be able to do a better job of holding this conversation with Tom if they use the PASTA process. Yet, they know it won't be easy. Tom is likely to react in any of the following ways:

- say his parents are making a big deal about nothing
- become angry with them
- point to inconsistencies in his parents' view of the world
- say that no-one else has such unreasonable parents
- blame and/or find fault
- tell his parents that his life will be ruined
- distract his parents by taking them on a tangent
- shirk responsibility: 'It's not my fault that this happened.'
- minimise: 'You're making a big drama out of nothing!'
- get angry and walk away
- argue that the changes his parents are suggesting will ruin his life
- say, 'It won't happen again', then continue on as before
- say, 'You want to blame me for everything!'

These are all *normal* reactions of a boy of Tom's age who is being confronted.

Tom is not a child with an oppositional behaviour problem, but like any human he's going find it tough to contain all his emotions when someone challenges his assumption that he can do what he wants. Serena and Charlie are trying to predict some of these responses and be ready to deal with them. When you need to hold a PASTA conversation with your children you'll probably want to do the same. And the whole thing isn't that hard if you're prepared.

But for now, let's cut to the chase and see how Serena and Charlie intend to hold a PASTA conversation with Tom at home.

P IS FOR … PREPARE

The first thing they need to do is work out what they will say. This is not a hard process, and once they've done it a few times they'll need less preparation. To start with, though, it's important to do the five steps in the preparation process so you get a rhythm going.

SERENA: I can't believe that Tom was up the other night playing that multiplayer game at two in the morning. It was a school night! What's going on with him? He knows better than that.

CHARLIE: Sometimes he's been up doing the phone thing as well. He's been well and truly pushing the boundaries with the screen stuff lately.

SERENA: I don't know … at one level, it's what a lot of boys his age are doing, but he's been an irritable little bugger lately. I reckon half of it's because he hasn't been sleeping properly.

CHARLIE: Well, look, I think we should have a talk with him. What do you say we organise to meet with him on Saturday? How about … at ten or so?

SERENA: Good idea.

CHARLIE: Well, who's going to tell him?

SERENA: I will. I'll line him up before I go to work in the morning.

CHARLIE: Maybe we can have a go with that PASTA script together?

SERENA: Yeah, good idea. I think we need to show him we're united on this.

The Blooms are onto the problem. They have some preparation worksheets from Dr Wiles (you'll find these at the end of the chapter).

The first thing they need to do is describe the problem they are facing using a simple formula called CPR. I first came across this in *Crucial Confrontations*, by Kerry Patterson and his colleagues. They suggest that all problems can be described by looking closer at three areas: content, pattern and relationship. Let's have a go.

- **Content**. The first stage is for Serena and Charlie to paint a picture of what the problem looks like from the outside, as if someone is looking at it from a distance. This is the *content* of the problem. Here they attempt to describe what they're going to say in objective third-person terms. The trick is to stay external — they need to simply paint a picture of the problem without any name-calling:

Tom is staying up late on school nights.[FACT]

Tom has been sending and receiving messages late at night when his parents think he is asleep.[FACT]

Tom is playing massive multiplayer games during the night with teenagers in other time zones. [FACT]

- **Pattern**. Often problems occur as part of a *pattern* that has been forming. Serena and Charlie think about the series of events that has led up to the problem with Tom. They describe this pattern:

Tom has been getting into a habit of playing adrenalin-pumping games right up and until his bedtime — with no wind-down time and no getting ready for sleep. This has been happening for three months now.

- **Relationships**. What we do in a family affects others. In Tom's case, his tiredness has been causing problems for nearly everyone. He is irritable, and he is getting cranky with his family all too frequently. The Blooms describe it like this:

Tom is irritable and cranky with everyone in the house. He is really stressing out his little sister by the way he is behaving. He is nearly always cranky with his mother.

decide on the bottom line, compromises and consequences

There are three more things to do in preparation for a tough conversation. Serena and Charlie need to work out:

1. What is their 'bottom line'? In other words, what just *can't* continue (for example, Tom not getting good sleep)?

2. What are they willing to compromise on (for example, times to meet and some curfews)?

3. What are the consequences of continued violation of the rules (for example, another tough conversation, confiscation of a phone or laptop for a time)?

They have to be clear about these matters beforehand so they know how they will respond if they arise.

A IS FOR ... ARRANGE AN APPOINTMENT

The time has come for Serena and Charlie to make a time to talk with Tom. Serena's nominated herself to organise the appointment.

Serena is ready to go to work and is calm as she intercepts Tom. She knows what she's going to say and has thought about what to do if Tom interrupts her.

SERENA: So, Tom, what have you got on at school today?

TOM: Mmm, it's Soph's birthday so they're doing a cake thing.

SERENA: Well, wish her a happy birthday from me. Before I go to work, I'd like to make a time to talk about the internet and a few things that have been happening at home lately.

TOM: [*Immediately defensive; he's tired*] What? Why do we have to do that? Why do we have to talk about it?

SERENA: [*Focused, not taking the bait, but finishing what she wants to say*] Tom, now's not a good time — I have to get to work. But your dad and I want to talk with you about some things we've been meaning to sort out for a while. So, I'd really like *you* to be part of that conversation. You're nearly a teenager now and it'll be good for you to negotiate some things with us. We can have some cake in the lounge room on Saturday at ten o'clock. OK?

TOM: [*Grimacing, rolling his eyes*] What's there to sort out?

SERENA: [*Calmly — she's not thrown by Tom's reaction*] Will ten on Saturday suit you?

TOM: Not ten. Joe and I are skating on Saturday.

SERENA: How about twelve o'clock? You should be home by then.

TOM: [*Grumbling, reluctant*] But Mum, I don't *get* it. Why do we have to do this?

SERENA: [*Ignoring Tom's pleading*] Why don't you have a think about what you want to say? We'll talk about it on Saturday at about twelve, with some cake.

Serena does well here. She doesn't try to have the conversation with Tom there and then. She tells Tom what she and Charlie want to discuss with him, and where and when it will happen. She stays calm throughout.

S IS FOR ... SAY SOMETHING AFFIRMING (1)

It's Saturday now. Serena, Charlie and Tom are in the lounge room, pouring tea and cutting a cake.

CHARLIE: [*Knowing he has to begin the conversation positively*] You right, Tom? Mum and I'd like to start, if you're ready. Good on ya, mate.

TOM: Do we *have* to do this? What's the big deal?

CHARLIE: Yes, mate, we have to. Look, the first thing I want say is you're not in trouble here. We think you're mostly doing really well at the moment. We like that you are going out and playing sport, and it's great that you're so interested in motorbikes.

TOM: [*Sighing, groaning*] How long's this going to take? I've got stuff to do ... y'know, like homework and ...

CHARLIE: [*Making a statement of common ground*] You're a great boy, Tom. Here's the thing, though: Mum and I are a bit concerned about how the internet is being used at home and we're wanting to change a few things so it can be used for all our benefits.

We all know the internet is a wonderful thing, as long as it's used well. Lately, though, we feel that the way you've been using the computer — and your phone — has been a bit of a problem. If we can agree about some things, we won't have to hassle you.

I'm sure you don't want us nagging you about this stuff, so I'm hoping we can work out an agreement between us. That way we can put this behind us and move on.

TOM: [*Sniping, attacking*] You just want to control me all the time. Why can't I live my own life?

CHARLIE: [*Staying focused and in control, not taking the bait*] Well, I guess you won't want me being in charge forever, but given that you are twelve, we still have a say for the moment.

Tom sits, fuming at having to go through this humiliating conversation.

Charlie's off to a good start here. He's said something kind about Tom. He's told Tom he's not in trouble, and that he and Serena want to talk about how he uses the internet at home.

S IS FOR … SAY WHAT THE PROBLEM IS (2)

CHARLIE: [*Unemotionally, in a matter-of-fact tone*] So, here's the problem, Tom. Since you got your new phone last month we've noticed that you have been getting messages late at night. The other thing that happened last week was that we went into your bedroom really late and you were playing a game on your laptop with some guys from Bolivia.

TOM: [*Clearly getting irritated*] So what, Dad! What's the big deal?

CHARLIE: Well, Tom, it was two in the morning, mate, and it was a school night.

TOM: School sucks!

Charlie doesn't lose his place or forget he hasn't quite finished describing the problem — he still needs to describe to Tom what he's sees about his irritability at home.

CHARLIE: I can see how you might think we are making a big deal out of this, Tom … but I haven't quite finished telling you what else your mum and I have been seeing at home. So, if you'll give me a bit more time, I would like to finish what I want to say.

The other thing we've noticed is that you've been pretty crabby at home lately. In fact, your blow-ups at your sister have been more frequent. Not good, mate. We think it's probably because you're not getting the sleep we think you need.

TOM: Oooawhh? Get real, you guys! What do you mean, 'not enough sleep'? I get heaps of sleep. This is crap. Who needs sleep anyway?

CHARLIE: [*Endeavouring not to get derailed by Tom's frustrations*] I know this is frustrating for you. But I'd like to get back to the topic. Can you try to hold it together a bit longer, and then I'll let you have your say?

Charlie's been interrupted a few times, but he hasn't lost his way. He knew he needed to get three things out: that Tom has been up late at night when he should have been sleeping; that he's been playing his games late at night; and that he's been irritable at home. Charlie has set the scene for describing what he wants.

S IS FOR … SAY WHAT YOU WANT (3)

'We've decided that we want three things'

CHARLIE: [*Getting back to the main things he wants to see changed*] So, Tom, Mum and I have talked about this problem and here's what we want from you. We've decided that we want three things.

One, we want everyone's phone and laptop to stay on the charger — in the kitchen — overnight.

Two, we want you to get one hour's down-time before you go to bed — no screens except on weekends and holidays. This means we want everybody off their screens by nine o'clock at night.

Three, we want you to aim to get eight and a half hours of sleep a night.

Tom's reaction is not good. He looks increasingly angry and resistant.

TOM: This is crap! You mean I can't take my phone to bed? My Facebook is none of your business! What is this, PRISON? You've been to another course, haven't you?

Charlie pauses, noticeably, to collect his thoughts.

Remember, we can expect that Tom will not be happy about what his parents want to change. But what Charlie does here is stay calm and not let himself be provoked by Tom's reaction. He stays focused on his part in the conversation and deals with Tom being upset. He is prepared. He knows he can afford to wait and he knows what he needs to say to deal with Tom's reactions.

T IS FOR ... TAME THE TIGER

CHARLIE: [*Making a reflective statement*] Tom, I can see you're feeling angry about this. I can see how you might feel like I'm fussing about nothing.

TOM: [*Still pretty angry*] But it's not fair — no other kid around here has parents like you guys. It's so unfair!

Tom arcs up, predicting the worst and still resistant, and building up a head of steam.

It *is*! You want to take away my phone. You're trying to stop me using Facebook. All you want to do is control me. No-one else's parents go on like this! You're *such* control freaks!

CHARLIE: [*Making a deeper reflective statement*] So, you think we're being too hard on you.

TOM: [*Looking noticeably righteous, and even angrier*] It's NOT FAIR. Why do I have to get punished for having a phone?

CHARLIE: We're not saying you can't use your phone — or Facebook. What we are saying is that we need to know that we all use the internet properly and we think that you have been staying up late and not getting enough sleep. We don't think that the way you have been using it has been in your best interests, Tom. That's it.

TOM: 'Best interests'? What's that supposed to mean? You just want to punish me.

CHARLIE: So you think we're trying to punish you for doing something that you're really interested in?

TOM: Yeah — you are! Bloody hell.

CHARLIE: Mum and I want to make sure you're safe and healthy. We want you to behave responsibly online and use your phone appropriately. We want to make sure you get enough sleep and are not too tired for school.

TOM: [*Snippy and snarling*] Right ... SLEEP! Oh, get *over* it! I GET ENOUGH SLEEP!

Serena decides she's going to say something. She does not get distracted or angry, and challenges Tom to take some responsibility.

SERENA: You feel annoyed because Dad and I want to set some limits. That's pretty normal. It's frustrating not being able to do what you want to do.

TOM: [*Upset, affronted and full of indignation*] Yeah, but ... what's going to happen to my games with the other guys overseas?

SERENA: Well, I'm sure you can get involved in some other games in the same time zone, Tom, so that you are not online late at night when it's daytime for the other gamers.

TOM: This is shit.

SERENA: I can see this is frustrating for you, Tom.

Again, Charlie and Serena keep on track with what they want to say. They continue to acknowledge what Tom may be feeling. While not agreeing with Tom, they stay where Tom is at emotionally (remember this from emotion coaching in the last chapter?) but at the same time they stay firm about what they want. They are ready for Tom's objections. Instead of getting into an argument with Tom, their preparation has put them in a better position to handle Tom's flare-ups. Charlie and Serena had thought through what they wanted. They make their reasons for wanting to change Tom's behaviour clear: he is not looking after himself, he is not sleeping enough and his tiredness is resulting in him getting angry with Jessica. Good job, parents!

A IS FOR ... AGREE

'OK, so this is what is going to happen ...'

CHARLIE: Well, Tom, we are really proud of you for at least talking with us about this problem. We realise that you are not so happy with what we are asking you to do. We have been concerned about your irritability at home and, in particular, your outbursts at your sister.

TOM: But this is *so* stupid.

Charlie lets this comment go through to the keeper.

CHARLIE: OK, so this is what is going to happen. We want you to organise things so you're in bed by ten o'clock on school nights. The second thing is that we will stop using any computer or phone screens by nine, unless there are exceptional circumstances. TV is fine after this time. At night, we will leave *all our phones* and laptops on the charger in the kitchen. In the New Year, we will review this plan to see where things are up to. We think these arrangements will help everyone be a bit more tolerant towards one another.

Charlie wraps up the meeting.

CHARLIE: Tom, Mum and I are really pleased that you can talk this through with us. We realise this is a big ask of you, but we need to see you not losing sleep to the internet. If things change in time, we may change what we have talked about today, but we will have another chat about that later on.

TOM: [*Thinking to himself 'As if!' but also half acknowledging what his parents have said*]. OK, OK! Can I go now?

SERENA: Yeah, sure. [*As Tom gets up to leave*] Thanks, Tom, you've done well.

Charlie and Serena stay calm and firm. There's no yelling and no blaming — just clear direction about *what* will happen at their house and *how* it will happen. Tom is not in charge and his parents need to take control when their son's behaviour is not in his best interests. Serena and Charlie hold firm and refuse to let Tom's reaction cause a problem. Even though Tom arcs up at various moments, they keep calm and collected, reflecting on the PASTA process and wending their way back and forth between Tom's objections and the script they wish to get through.

There's no need to panic — they know they'll get there. Just like a sailing boat that has to tack between positions to get to its destination when the wind is against it, Charlie and Serena navigate towards a solution to resolve Tom's unacceptable behaviour — all quite effectively and calmly.

Charlie and Serena stay calm throughout, even though they find it pretty challenging to not react to some of Tom's outbursts. Remember back in chapter 7 when we looked at how managing ourselves is a key part of managing our children's behaviour? Well, you can see how this works in a PASTA conversation. Although Charlie and Serena find it hard, they are able to control their feelings and keep their bigger goal in mind — to resolve Tom's unacceptable behaviour. By behaving this way, and not flying off the handle, Charlie and Serena have modelled to their children that problems need not always be resolved though yelling and berating but by following a process, and by doing a bit of planning. If this type of strategy is used to resolve problems with their children as they reach their teenage years it will be less stressful for everyone concerned. The trick here is to begin before their children become teenagers so that this process becomes part of the pattern of what happens in their family.

SET UP YOUR OWN PASTA CONVERSATION — A GUIDE MAP

Over the next few pages I'll go through each step in a PASTA conversation. Remember, it doesn't matter what the problem is — you can use PASTA to keep you on track. Then, at the end of the chapter, you'll find worksheets you can use to prepare your PASTA conversation. When you've filled them in, I suggest practising the conversation with a friend. This will better prepare you for your child's reactions.

A big part of successfully tackling a difficult issue with your child is how you conduct yourself when you're having a tough conversation with them. There are three main points to this:

- decide that you will not lose your temper or retaliate

- don't blame your child for upsetting you

- relax, and let go of the idea that you have to get it exactly right.

If your child doesn't settle after you've attempted to deal with their objections, then call it off (postpone to another day) or ask them to pull themselves up so you can continue or enact the consequence you have decided on. In other words, you have responses you can put in place. The important thing here is that if we expect our children to self-regulate, we have to as well, and that involves us going into the conversation in the right headspace — no angst, no spoiling for a fight and no getting angry. You don't need to. All you need to do is work to your script.

P IS FOR ... PREPARE

Your purpose in the preparation stage is to *write your script*. Once you've had a few PASTA conversations with your children, you probably won't need to prepare so much, but for the first time it's essential so that you don't lose your place or get sidetracked.

First, think about the problem using CPR, and consider its:

- *content* (describe it objectively)

- *pattern* (think about how it keeps emerging, if it does)

- effect on *relationships* (look at how it is negatively affecting trust and co-operation).

Second, consider:

- What's your bottom line?

- What are you willing to compromise on?

- What are the consequences of not agreeing to the bottom line?

  – withdrawal of privileges

  – imposed limitations (e.g. reduction of internet time).

A IS FOR … ARRANGE AN APPOINTMENT

Your purpose here is to signal the issue with your child. You don't want to have the conversation then and there. Rather, it should be a formal appointment that's not rushed or done in a hurry.

- Do it at a time when you or your child are leaving or going somewhere. The idea is to put off having a PASTA conversation so that you have time to prepare, and so that there is some formality to what you are doing. You are trying to establish a new pattern of more structured and calmer negotiation, rather than rushed hallway conversations, or people standing and screaming at one another.

- Tell them what you want to talk about

- Tell them where your meeting will be

- Give them a time for your meeting

- Tell them you'll want to hear from them

From the original dialogue between Serena and Tom you'll remember this.

Before I go to work, I'd like to make a time to talk with you about the internet and a few things that have been happening at home lately. We'd like to meet at five this afternoon in the lounge room. Dad and I want to say a few things and we'd like to hear from you too.

S IS FOR SAY …
SAY SOMETHING AFFIRMING

Your purpose is to start off on an affirming note.

- 'The first thing I want to say to you is how proud we are that you're here; it shows great maturity …'

- 'Good on you for being here. I'm really impressed …'

- 'I want to start off by saying that I am really happy that you are here …'

- 'We love you very much and we think you are a beautiful person …'

- 'One of the good things we know about you is …'

- 'We can see how mature you are becoming when you show us you can talk this through …'

From the original dialogue, here's how it went;

> *Look, the first thing I want to say is that you're not in trouble here. We think you're mostly doing really well at the moment. We like that you're going out and playing sport …*

SAY what the problem is

Think back to your CPR preparation, where you objectively described the content of the problem, the pattern of the problem and how it affects relationships. Now is when you need to explain the problem to your child using simple language, without emotion or emotive language. You'll notice, importantly, that Charlie states these matters as 'facts'. There's no embellishments, no name-calling and no insults.

From the original script:

> *So, here's the problem, Tom. Since you got your new phone last month we've noticed that you have been getting messages late at night. [FACT]*

> *… we went into your bedroom really late and you were playing a game on your laptop with some guys from Bolivia. [FACT]*

*... we've have noticed that you've been pretty crabby at home lately.
[FACT]*

To get started with this type of description, you need to use phrases like:

- 'Let me start off by telling you *what's been happening* lately ...'

- 'I want to tell you what we have *seen* happening ...'

- 'We have *noticed* that you ...'

- 'We have *heard* you saying ...'

- 'I just want to replay what I *saw* happen ...'

- 'I'd like to *describe* to you what I reckon has been happening lately ...'

- 'If I can start by *reflecting on what happened* the other day ...'

SAY what you want

Your purpose here is to tell your child what you want to see happen in the future. From the original script:

So, Tom, Mum and I have talked about this problem and here's what we want from you. We've decided that we want three things.

One, we want everyone's phone to stay on the charger — in the kitchen — overnight.

Two, we want you to get one hour's down-time before you go to bed — no screens except on weekends and holidays. This means we want everybody off their screens by nine o'clock at night.

Three, we want you to aim to get eight and a half hours of sleep a night.

T IS FOR ... TAME THE TIGER

Your purpose here is to deal with your child's frustration or anger, and attempt to calm them if they arc up. If you expect your child will not necessarily like what you have to say, you can have responses ready. When they interrupt, remember to bookmark, pause, then:

- say what you 'see' happening for them
- imagine what they're feeling and say it to them

Remember, you're the paramedic here. You're attempting to stay detached. You can slow the conversation down, and go with their feelings to calm them down or help them feel safe again (as in the previous chapter on emotion coaching). Using the sailing analogy again, you can tack, and then return to PASTA. You know where you're going. You just need to bookmark where you're up to. If your child interrupts you, go back to the PASTA process after you've heard them out. With most kids this is all you'll have to do. Listen to what they're feeling to help them toggle and then, after a silence, re-enter PASTA where you left off.

Reflective listening statements might start with the following:

- 'So, what I hear you saying is ...'
- 'I'm guessing that you feel like we are ...'
- 'Seems to me that you're ...'
- 'If I was you, I would have felt pretty [angry] about that too ...'
- 'What I'm seeing is that you're ...'
- 'Looks to me you're feeling really frustrated that ...'
- 'Sitting here, looking at you, I'm thinking that ...'

In other words, if you tame the tiger correctly (by staying in the 'feeling moment'), it should work to reduce the intensity of the feelings they are experiencing. This act of really being heard is enough to help them get back into being rational so you can progress with the PASTA script and solve the problem.

Remember, if it all goes pear-shaped, you can bail out. Unfortunately, some children do get into the habit of letting their anger rage unbridled, and they can't be settled by good reflective listening. Instead, these children are probably in the habit of menacing their parents. Again, the first thing for you to remember is to keep your cool. You have options: you can challenge your child to get control, or tell them you'll have the conversation with them later when they are prepared to discuss the problem more calmly. Alternatively, you can apply consequences.

So, in summary, if you have temporarily put aside your PASTA agenda to really 'hear' what your child is experiencing, and you've made four or five really good reflective comments but your child is simply not calming down, you'll need to say something to ask them to assume self-control. Something like:

> I have really tried to hear how frustrating this is for you. I'd like to go on to solve the problem we are having but I can't unless you are able to calm yourself. Do you think you can get calmer or should we put this off until tomorrow?

In other words, you have *really* tried hard to listen, the conversation can't continue for now unless they settle. What you're asking them to do is regroup so you can go on, or giving the option of having the conversation another day.

If this fails to tame the tiger, you will need to go to plan B: let it go for today. Next time you meet, though, you'll need to remind your child that it's important for you to explain things, and that their menacing behaviour last time was unacceptable. Make it clear that they will have to demonstrate some self-control if you are to negotiate a good outcome.

Being clear about your bottom line and what you are willing to compromise on (e.g. the time of the meeting, and what will happen as a consequence) will give you great clarity in considering what you will do if an outcome cannot be negotiated. Try to set up another conversation first (remember, this is new to you both) and, if this doesn't work, apply your bottom-line consequence (e.g. taking away their phone for the day).

A IS FOR … AGREE

Your final task is to describe your agreement. If you can name what's in it for your child as well as yourself, that's good:

- 'I want to wrap up what I think we've agreed …'

- 'OK, let's look at what we've been talking about …'

- 'If I were to summarise what I reckon we've agreed, I'd say …'

- 'Let me recap what I think we're agreeing about …'

From the original:

> OK, so this is what is going to happen. We want you to organise things so you're in bed by ten o'clock on school nights. The second thing is that we will stop using any computer or phone screens by nine, unless there are exceptional circumstances. TV is fine after this time. At night, we will leave all our phones and laptops on the charger in the kitchen. In the New Year, we will review this plan to see where things are up to. We think these arrangements will help everyone be a bit more tolerant towards one another.

PREPARE YOUR OWN PASTA CONVERSATION

The next few pages contain a blank worksheet you can use to set up your PASTA conversation. Preparing what you are going to say is a very important part of the process.

So, where to next?

So far we've looked at some ways to identify, sort out and deal with our children's difficult behaviour and to change those BIG ROCKS. PASTA conversations give us a way to deal with those behaviours that aren't being resolved in any other way. In the next chapter we'll shift gears a little and look at how we can encourage the behaviours we *want* to see — by building bonds with children and teaching them how to master new skills and ways to maintain behaviour you want to see more often.

POSTSCRIPT ON THE BLOOMS' TOUGH CONVERSATION WITH TOM

Nowadays, the Blooms are in the habit of having down-time before going to bed at night. Each night all phones and laptops go into the charging basket in the kitchen. Tom was initially crabby and unhappy about surrendering his phone each night, but his sleep has improved and there are no midnight blips from the iPhone. Instead, now that it's clear that the iPhone and his laptop stay in the charging basket overnight, Tom's behaviour in particular has improved. He's less provocative towards Jessica and he's less irritable all round. Charlie and Serena know this problem was not going to go away by itself. Holding the PASTA conversation helped them resolve Tom's difficult behaviour without them having to resort to punishing or coercing him.

PASTA WORKSHEET

PREPARE

What is the problem, in a few words? Describe it in terms of its content, pattern and how it affects relationships. Refer back to the Blooms' worksheet, if that helps.

content — what has happened, in objective, factual terms?

_____

_____

pattern — how has it been reoccurring?

_____

_____

relationships — how does it affect those close to your child?

_____

_____

What is your bottom line, i.e. the consequence if you cannot negotiate with your child?

_____

_____

What are you willing to compromise on?

_____

_____

What are the consequences for your child if they do not follow the agreement you reach?

- withdrawal of privileges?
- imposed limitations (e.g. withdrawal of internet use for a week)?

ARRANGE AN APPOINTMENT

Do this at a time when you or your child are going somewhere.

The appointment will be at _____ (time) on _____(day)

in _____ (location).

Write down what you are going to say:

_____

_____

_____

_____

_____

_____

_____

SAY ... SOMETHING AFFIRMING

Be kind in your initial approach.

Write down what you are going to say:

_____

_____

_____

_____

_____

_____

_____

_____

SAY ... WHAT THE PROBLEM IS

Be clear, objective and factual, and do not use emotive language.

Write down what you are going to say:

_____

_____

_____

_____

_____

_____

_____

SAY ... WHAT YOU WANT

Describe exactly what you want from your child.

Write down what you are going to say:

_____

_____

_____

_____

_____

_____

_____

_____

TAME THE TIGER

Remember to bookmark, pause ... then reflect on what they might be experiencing, call them to attention or say what you see.

Write down what you are going to say:

_____

_____

_____

_____

_____

_____

_____

AGREE

Tell them what you think you have agreed on.

Write down what you are going to say:

_____

_____

_____

_____

_____

_____

_____

in essence

- Some problems with your children will require you to sit down and confront their behaviour by having a *conversation* about it. These may be problems you've been ignoring for a while but that have now settled into patterns that you would like to change.

- PASTA is a method for *holding a tough conversation* with older children (aged ten and over) about 'big-ticket' behaviour problems.

- PASTA stands for *prepare, appointment, say, tame the tiger* and *agree*.

- The PASTA method assumes that your child may *get upset* or arc up at you, and offers a set of strategies for staying calm, focused and on track.

- To do PASTA well initially, it's important to *prepare*. Clarify the problem using CPR (content, pattern, relationship), think about how your child may react, write out what you're going to say (using preparation worksheets) and practise on a friend if you can.

CHAPTER 11
building bonds, teaching skills and encouraging competency

Earlier on in this book, we went to some trouble to identify the wanted behaviour that we see in our children. We included a list of behaviours that we want to teach, show and encourage in our children. Do you remember this list from the Blooms' behaviour sorting worksheet back in chapter 4?

- clean room on Saturday
- brush teeth each night
- take bag to room after school
- clean up toys after play
- put clothes on for school
- take dirty clothes to laundry.

I have often looked at parents' WANTED lists and find the same sort of behaviours keep appearing – that is, behaviours that need *teaching*. To build up our children's ability to do these tasks, we have to actively show them how. They are behaviours that need to be 'put together' for children, from the simplest task right up to the competency required to do the task from beginning to end. Teaching these skills involves:

- breaking the tasks into steps
- helping children link the behaviour pieces to one another
- keeping them interested in persisting with the skill.

When we teach children the skills we'd like to see them use, we are not just rewarding them for any behaviour, we are *connecting* parts of the behaviour together for them, and keeping them motivated for the future.

TEACHING OUR CHILDREN WANTED BEHAVIOURS

There are three steps to teaching our children the behaviours we'd like to see more of:

1. model what we want done

2. break the behaviour into its parts so we can teach the parts and string them together

3. help them chain parts of the behaviour together to achieve overall competency.

At the beginning of the preschool year, all around Australia preschool teachers show children how to unpack their bags and store their belongings. At first the teachers show the children what they want them to do using a series of easy-to-remember steps: unpack their bags, put their lunches in a particular place and so on, in a particular order. The teacher goes through what she wants them to do, step by step, to get the job done.

Every day after that, the preschoolers go through their 'arrival' routine — they do the same thing each day, en masse. Soon enough, they learn what is expected. They learn all these mini-tasks, put them together in a sequence, and *voila*! The children do this as a part of their day with no rewards and no praise. They feel good that they can do this job, they feel secure in the routine and they do it in unison with their group. They do this routine because 'this is what we do' at preschool.

When you teach children tasks you want to see more of, you'll need to keep two things in mind: first, it's important to make it easy for them to do; and second, you need to keep them motivated so they will continue to do the tasks in the future, and enjoy for themselves the satisfaction of getting the job done.

Obviously, for example, we can't expect three-year-olds to brush their teeth unaided, so we mostly do it for them. But as we get them into the routine of cleaning their teeth, we might also set it up so that they do certain other parts of the task. You know, it's kind of sensible to get them to squeeze the toothpaste onto the brush at some point. Then, as they get better at doing that, we might add other parts that they can do, such as brushing up and down on their front teeth, then making sure that they have cleaned all the teeth inside their mouth.

Because much of our self-esteem has to do with doing things well, we are much better off teaching children how to be competent.

PRAISE AND REWARDS

Change experts — whose job it is to investigate how we can positively affect behaviour in other people — have a lot to say about how to encourage people's behaviour. They tend to agree that the best way to encourage people to continue to do a task is to help them assume mastery over that task (so they feel good about being able to do something well) and to maintain that behaviour (by harnessing support from others in the group). *This* is how we can encourage our children in their WANTED behaviours. Not everything needs to be linked to a reward, and not everything has to be fun. It's called life and it can be maintained by making the task easy to do and by making it part of the values we share.

So, here's my view on praise: I think we use praise too much as a means to encourage our children to do what we would like them to do when we could use it more effectively. What we should be doing is using praise or rewards as *adjuncts* to teaching skills, not as the main strategy. Externally delivered praise and rewards do *not* teach children competency or necessarily give them the self-satisfaction that comes when a job has been done well. It is by teaching and showing our children how to do the tasks we'd like to see that they attain competency. Praise and rewards do have a role, though — when used carefully — to encourage children to keep practising these skills and eventually master them. But if we use praise and rewards all the time they will lose their power as motivators.

I know it's important for us to be positive with our children, but I also believe that praise and rewards are overused in parenting literature. Simply applying, say, a 5:1 ratio of praise to negative comments, as I have seen suggested in countless parenting books, is too simplistic. Sure, we *should* use fewer negative comments to describe our children's behaviour — I agree. But we should also try to encourage or praise our children to best affect their behaviour, which is not about just applying a ratio. When we overuse praise and rewards from the *outside-in*, we can sometimes lessen an *inside-out* goal — the self-satisfying impact of a job well done. The inside-out benefit should be our main focus, not just gaining compliance from our children because they expect some reward.

Praise, then, is meaningless if it's applied willy-nilly. If you're going to use it, it's best to think about when and how it will have the biggest impact. You can use it strategically to promote 'vital' behaviours you want to see more of, and use it strategically and sparingly to achieve better results. Do you know why poker machines are addictive? Because they reward people *every now and then*. That's it. The person wanting the win doesn't get it every time, only occasionally. I don't want to talk you out of using rewards and praise. Rather it's *how* they're used that I want you to pay attention to.

Essentially, I want to draw your attention to the importance of building up a sense that doing a job well is its own reward. We feel good not only because someone else tells us that we are doing well, but because we *believe* we can do the task, and because we are part of a group that does the same thing. If our children know that many of the things they do are part of 'what we do around here' (and don't do), they will feel the need to be part of that group and act accordingly.

If our children can do tasks and master skills for themselves *and* feel like they are part of a group, these two factors will sustain their efforts better than if they are overpraised. There's lots of evidence to show that carefully applied praise will help our children do more of what we want them to do, but praise should be third in the hierarchy — after, one, learning how to do something and feeling good about being able to do it, and two, feeling supported by their group or tribe (the family). If, in the process of doing what they do, our children are intrinsically rewarded (they feel good about themselves) *and* they receive confirmatory messages from the people with whom they are attached, they will be more likely to maintain this behaviour.

WE CAN USE PRAISE TO ENCOURAGE OUR CHILDREN TO STEP UP

Once children have learnt the basics of how to do something, it's important to help them stay motivated and practise their behaviours until they become second nature. Children will need some supports to motivate them to *want* to get better and better at new skills. This is where carefully applied praise and rewards fit into the picture. Here are some tips.

- Do things you want your children to do in groups: clean together, cook together and even brush your teeth together!

- When you do use praise, make sure it is linked to an improvement in the wanted behaviour you're hoping to see. Instead of saying, 'You're such a good boy,' say instead, 'I noticed you have been taking the veggie scraps out to the compost when you've been doing your kitchen clean-up. I like the way that you've been getting the whole job done lately.'

- Try to notice the process of how things get done, and the effort involved, *not* just the finished product. Instead of saying, 'Your painting is great! What a terrific artist you are!' you could say, 'I can see that you really *tried* hard with that painting. I'm really happy you did that.'

- Try to create a fun game out of what you ask your children to do: 'I'm going to set the timer for fifteen minutes. I reckon we can do the washing-up and get dressed and be out to the car in that time. What do you say?'

- Notice things about what your children do: 'I haven't had to ask you to take your plate out to the sink all this week. I think that deserves a mini-celebration. Let's go out for an ice-cream tomorrow night.' The effort by a parent that makes the 'invisible visible' is often overlooked, but it's really important to say what we see happening when we see it.

- Notice your children when they play co-operatively with each other: 'I like the way you two are taking turns in that game.'

- Send text messages to your child, telling them about a great job they've done.

- Write a message on a sticky note about how much you appreciated something your child has done, and put it in their lunchbox or on their pillow.

- Brag about something your child did well in front of a friend: 'You know, I'm so proud of Matty for regularly feeding our dog. He's been doing it every night without fail.'

- Older children appreciate being given some time to get things done, especially if they are in the middle of a game or their favourite show on TV. For instance, 'Tom, can you take the garbage after *Neighbours* is finished?' or 'Matty, I need you to unpack the dishwasher before you have a shower. Thanks, mate.'

- If children receive pocket money, you can tell them that if they don't do their jobs, you'll do them instead but you'll also deduct an amount from their pocket money each time you have to do this.

BUILD BONDS WITH YOUR CHILDREN

In every situation in our lives, there are expectations. We expect things of one another in the workplace, in community settings and at home. As we live and work together we are bound by often invisible codes about appropriate or inappropriate behaviour. There's often a tension between what we want to do as individuals and what's good for our family, but let's make no bones about it — whether we like it or not, we *are* affected by those we live and work with.

While we want our children to feel good about what they do and achieve, it's also the case that we should encourage them to collaborate and try to adhere to our family values. Some of these values involve putting off what they want as individuals and showing compassion to one another — not necessarily for a reward, but because that's what being part of a family means. It's entirely reasonable to expect that some behaviour should just occur because that's the way it is. In some cases it's important to express pleasure or to reward a child for a job well done, but there are other ways for us to teach our children to value and get along with others.

When you want to motivate your children to keep on doing particular things or demonstrating particular behaviours, they are more likely to want to do this if they feel connected with you. This attachment between children and their parents happens for most children as a result of living together and depending on their parents. In my opinion, children will be more motivated to do what is needed the more strongly they feel part of a group that does things together.

If we want our children to be motivated to fit in with what we want from them, it's important that we maintain our relationship with them. Ultimately it's having a relationship with warm and firm parents that will make the biggest difference to a child's well-being and how they will respond to our encouragement of their behaviour.

A big part of identifying ABNS in chapter 4 is to consciously identify the behaviour you are going to actively overlook. By ignoring certain behaviour you are protecting your relationship with your children and preserving your attachment, instead of potentially eroding your relationship with them.

Here are some ideas for maintaining and building on your attachment with your children.

1. Regularly signpost the comings and goings in your life with your kids.

   – As they leave or you leave, tell them you love them.

   – When they go, say goodbye and give them a hug or a kiss.

    – After absences say, 'It's so good to see you!'

    – At breakfast, ask them, 'What are you up to today?'

2. Regularly express interest in what they say and do, even if it sounds a bit crazy.

    – Be curious, as often as you can, without judging.

    – Ask them to tell you the best thing about their day, and what didn't go so well.

    – Talk to them about their special interests.

    – If they express views that seem weird or unreal, consider if you can go along with them.

    – Generally speaking, it's not a good idea to knock your children's 'hope' on the head.

3. Ask them to show you what parts of a task they think they can do.

    – 'I'm wondering if you can show me how you can brush your teeth?'

    – 'You took your bag to the bedroom yesterday — can you show me where you put it?'

    – 'You baked a lovely cake; I think it looks just like the one in the picture.'

4. Join them in moments of happiness and sadness.

    – 'I can see you look happy about having tidied your room so neatly.'

    – 'It's such a delight to see you so happy about getting such good results!'

    – 'You look sad about your bird dying. I feel sad too.'

5. Make the physical environment work for you.

    – Have dinner at the table — not scattered around the living room. It may be the only time you come together all day so make the dining table a tool for doing this. Make dinner a screen-free zone (no phones, no TV, etc.).

– Prepare meals with each other.

– Shop with one another — dads, too. It builds bonds.

6. Give children (over seven) pocket money — there's a relationship in money.

– Give children some money for being part of your family — which they get no matter what.

– See that some money is tied to doing jobs — taking the garbage out or doing the vacuuming. Sometimes having this supplementary money in small change in one jar, with a separate jar for the jobs *you* have done for them, is effective because they can see their own pocket money decreasing as the money in your jar increases.

7. Plan fun times together as a family.

– Buy a calendar and let everyone take a turn choosing a family activity one Sunday a month.

– When you spend time with your children, do it on their terms. Get involved in their sport as a coach or a team manager or just to wash the shirts.

– Have a movie night, family picnics.

– Start up a ritual such as having pizzas on Friday nights — maybe in front of the TV

THIS ATTACHMENT IS IMPORTANT AS OUR CHILDREN GET OLDER, TOO

In his book *The 7 habits of highly effective people*, Stephen Covey talks about the importance of spending enjoyable time with your family, which he calls 'putting credits' in an emotional bank account. He says we can draw back on this 'credit' if we need to when we are trying to influence our children's behaviour. This is nowhere more important than in their teenage years, when we rely even more on having a good relationship with our children.

the future

As children grow older, your attempts to influence them will increasingly rely on:

- your relationship with them

- the enjoyable times you have shared

- your demonstration of respect for them and their goals.

In the end, it's my view that you're better off spending more time doing things that build bonds with your children and that improve your relationship with one another, than you are using too many rewards or treats. Spending time together doing fun things is essential to maintaining your relationship, and will count for more as they move into adolescence.

in essence

- The behaviours we usually want to see in our children are often behaviours that need *teaching*.

- Teaching these behaviours involves breaking the tasks into *steps* and helping children *link* the behaviour pieces to one another in a chain.

- When we teach children the behaviours we want to see, we need to make them *easy* and keep children *motivated* so they continue to do these tasks.

- We should not overuse outside-in *praise and rewards* to have our children do certain tasks. The aim is to encourage the inside-out benefit of children gaining *satisfaction* from a job well done, in doing things because this is *what we do*.

- Carefully applied praise can be used to motivate children to want to *practise* and improve their new skills, but should not be used to *teach* the skills in the first place.

- Children are more likely to want to keep on doing the things you would like them to do if their behaviour happens in the context of their *relationship* with you and with the 'tribe'/family. The *attachment* relationship of parent and child is central to this.

- If our children can *see the value in doing something for themselves* and feel like they are *part of a group*, these two factors will sustain their efforts better than if they are overpraised.

CHAPTER 12
bringing it all together and thinking about the future

Throughout *this book*, I have been encouraging the idea that we should be *selective* about how we parent. We *can* make choices. We *can* be mindful of what we are doing at various parenting moments and, in doing so, help our children achieve maturity. With some knowledge about how our children's brains develop, and a good set of strategies always in our minds, we can help our children practise using their mental brakes and, eventually, regulate their own behaviour so we don't have to intervene so much. That's our aim.

By now you will have seen that this book's general approach is to use some *outside-in* levers to encourage children's *inside-out* abilities (to manage their own behaviour). I'm sure that there are more options for helping children become happy and healthy, and this is *not* a book that presumes to cover all the possibilities for parenting. Instead, I've aimed to give you a simple model for dealing with your children's *difficult* behaviour. In my experience, this is why most parents get help.

In the vast, confusing and ever-more-crowded sea of opinions about how to manage children's behaviour, I have attempted to throw you a lifeline and show you a few options for dealing with difficult behaviour, keeping your available options to a minimum. If you can learn a few simple strategies and understand why they work, you will have mastered a basic toolkit to get you out of trouble.

Of course you may wish to build further on your repertoire of skills for parenting, and there are some very good books and resources around for you to do some more research. I've included some of my favourites in the back of the book, and listed some websites that offer some great advice. There are also a few more resources in the final part of this book — a self-test, some ideas on dealing with sleep issues, and notes about managing children and technology.

HELPING CHILDREN LEARN SELF-REGULATION — FROM THE INSIDE-OUT

We know there is evidence to support the view that children can be taught impulse control. We know that children are not automatically born with a good understanding of their social bearings. They are not as good as adults at balancing their emotions or at organising how they will respond to frustrations, but as they grow they become more skilled and there's much we can do to help them improve these abilities.

We know it's not always appropriate to let our feelings 'hang out', and there are some occasions when children need us to interpret the social world for them, particularly when it comes to hurting others or behaving rudely. And, forgiving as we need to be, there are also limits that everyone, including our children, simply have to get used to. If they grow up believing that they can 'lose it' when someone confronts them or they feel frustrated, they probably won't be able to do well at school, keep a job or stay in long-term relationships for very long.

We can help our children develop this self-regulation by keeping calm, managing ourselves, and managing their difficult behaviour quietly. All the strategies we have talked about in this book are non-violent ways to help our children achieve self-control. Practising these skills — and knowing that they *can* control their impulses — will stand them in good stead for other times when they will need to use their minds, such as when they might feel depressed or anxious. Practice will allow their brains to develop the pathways that will allow them to hesitate before they overreact. This is good news.

TALK LESS, LISTEN MORE IS A TRANSITION PLAN FOR CHANGE

I hope this book has helped you develop a plan for your family to change its unhelpful patterns. We've looked at how we can modify the way we deal with our children's difficult behaviour, tried to work out how we might be consciously or unconsciously contributing to what is happening, and also thought about ways to manage ourselves in the service of helping our children achieve self-regulation.

Being able to clearly see the patterns in our families that may contribute to our children's difficult behaviour is such an important step. Techniques such as sorting behaviour into ABNS, WANTED, UNWANTED and BIG ROCKS can help us achieve this clarity, because we can identify what our children do and decide what we need to do about it. Why get into arguments about things that don't matter? Why not save our energy for dealing with those serious behaviours that we *really* want our children to stop?

As we've seen, there *are* ways — achievable, easy-to-remember ways — to minimise arguments, stop misbehaviour escalating and maximise our children's co-operation. They start when we make smart choices about our children's behaviour. We can ignore it, stop it (by signalling), or emotion-coach it (if it has not escalated into a BIG ROCK). If the behaviour is part of a long-standing pattern, and our children are older than ten, we can address it using a PASTA conversation. And if it's a WANTED behaviour, we can teach our children to repeat it by breaking it down into steps, and maintain it by encouraging them to practise.

All the options and strategies in this book target the same objective: to model self-control and to help your children develop self-regulation. That's your mission: to change destructive patterns, increase your children's well-being, and look after the overall health of your family. And you *can* do it.

PART 5.
extra resources

test your know-how

the three choices model (see chapters 6 to 9) is a way of dealing with difficult behaviour on the run. It provides you with three quick options that you can choose from, according to the behaviour you see:

- If the behaviour is annoying but not serious (ABNS), you can overlook it.

- If the behaviour is a BIG ROCK, or something you want your children to stop, you signal (count) it.

- If the behaviour is an emotional response and has not yet escalated, you use emotion coaching to help your child gain a better understanding of their feelings and to manage their own behaviour.

I'm keen for you to try your new list of options for managing your children's behaviour. I do this at most of the parenting groups I run. Let's see if you can test yourself.

how to decide what to do

- Is it an ABNS — annoying but not serious? **Ignore it.**

- Is it a BIG ROCK behaviour? **Count it.**

- Is it a problem that hasn't escalated? **Emotion-coach it.**

WHAT TO DO WHEN …

Jessica, aged five, is annoying her older brother by knocking over his Lego building. Her brother has not seen her doing this yet, but Jessica's behaviour is obvious to you. What do you do?

☐ IGNORE IT?   ☐ COUNT?   ☐ EMOTION COACH?

Matty, aged seven, has come home from school complaining about his teacher, Mrs Fosby. According to Matty, Mrs Fosby made the whole class stay in at lunchtime when the same old kids were mucking up. He's really upset and angry, and feels unfairly treated. What do you do?

☐ IGNORE IT?   ☐ COUNT?   ☐ EMOTION COACH?

Tom, aged twelve, wants to go to a sleepover that 'all' his friends are going to. You've told him that you'll make a final decision once you've spoken to the parents whose child is having the sleepover. Tom wants an answer straight away and keeps badgering you. What do you do?

☐ IGNORE IT?   ☐ COUNT?   ☐ EMOTION COACH?

Tom, aged twelve, confronts his younger brother for using his MP3 player without asking. They yell at each other and Tom ends up hitting his brother. What do you do?

☐ IGNORE IT?   ☐ COUNT?   ☐ EMOTION COACH?

Matty, aged seven, is upset with his father. His dad had promised to take Matty and a friend to Sea World but now is unable to do so because something important has come up. Matty's dad is normally reliable, so Matty is bitterly disappointed. He has been complaining incessantly, but has not yet escalated to the point of rudeness. What do you do?

☐ IGNORE IT?   ☐ COUNT?   ☐ EMOTION COACH?

Matty: Emotion coach
Tom: Count a straight three
Tom: Count; it's a big rock
Matty: Emotion coach: it's not a big rock
Jessica: Count; it's a big rock
ANSWERS

children and technology

When we teach parents about technology at home, I refer to the internet as 'an invited guest, not an assumed resident'. This ultimately means that we may not be able to control what happens 'out there' on the net, but we can control what happens in our homes — and we should, because it has big implications for protecting our children's mental and physical well-being. Increasingly, we are finding that our children's well-being is affected if we don't take steps to manage their 'screen time' — their use of mobile phones, the internet (including social networking sites such as Facebook) and the way they use technology.

While the internet should not be seen as the bogeyman here — it has many fantastic features, such as education, communication, entertainment and online communities — its use can also have detrimental effect on our children's well-being if we do not engage with *how* they are using it. In my opinion, these big-ticket items affecting children's well-being are:

- lack of sleep and downtime to help their minds recuperate

- the depersonalising of children's relationships with one another

- the digital footprint unknowingly set down by children and young people which can affect their future.

SLEEP CAN BE DISRUPTED BY LATE-NIGHT SCREEN TIME

We all require certain amounts of sleep to function properly. Children need to get to bed on time and develop a 'going to sleep' routine that helps them get proper rest, or they will undermine their healthy development and their ability to cope at school.

Teenagers, for example, need an average of eight and a half hours sleep a night. That means that if they are getting up at 7am to get ready for school, they need to be in bed by 10.30pm on most nights. Research suggests that we need an hour away from screens (not including TVs, which emit a different light) for the melatonin in our systems to reach the right level for us to go off to sleep. (Melatonin is a hormone that plays a central role in our sleep-wake cycle.) This means that teenagers should be off their screens — phones, laptops, iPads, etc — by 9.30pm. How often do you think this is happening around our country? Not much, according to some experts, who say that most teenagers get less than seven hours sleep a night. Lack of sleep, as we know, results in our children feeling irritable, grumpy and foggy-headed, which impedes their learning.

Therefore, if I was to give one major reason to get involved in your children's screen time, it would be to ensure they get the right amount of sleep. If you want to find out some more information on this topic there is a lot available online. Search for the term 'sleep hygiene' or go to the Sleep Health Foundation website listed in the additional resources at the back of this book.

THE ONLINE ENVIRONMENT DEPERSONALISES OUR COMMUNICATION

In recent years much has been made about the major threat of online predators who target children via the internet, and how we need to protect our children from them. Although there are instances of this problem, there are two thoughts I will share with you: first, most young people are pretty savvy when it comes to weird people trying to lure them into bad scenes; second, the major threat to children and young people online is not predators, but the way young people treat each other. Bullying and destructive relationships are a much bigger problem than online predators.

There are two ways to approach this problem:

1. Make sure your children know how to protect themselves from online bullying. Let them know that it is OK for them to show you

messages they don't feel good about, and teach them that it's not always smart to respond in kind by insulting someone in return.

2. Try not to overreact. Some children fear that if they say there is a problem their parents will take them off the internet or ban them. Tell them they won't be banned and that you can sort out the problem together.

3. Help children develop some rules of thumb for posting messages on the internet — 'If you wouldn't say it to your grandma, don't send it' and 'Sleep on it — see if you feel the same way in the morning.' This will help them think about what they're doing before they send something they might regret.

LAYING DOWN A DIGITAL FOOTPRINT CAN AFFECT OUR REPUTATIONS

Many children don't think about the consequences of their behaviour — not because they are being reckless, but because the part of their brains that controls their long-range forecasting ability is still being built. That means that they can and will post things online that they may later regret.

These days, more and more employers and institutions are looking at prospective employees' social networking profiles and internet trails before choosing who gets a job. While many of us may never fully get our heads around why many young people live such public lives on the internet rather than take pride in their privacy, I am still convinced we can help them protect themselves by setting up appropriate privacy settings on Facebook and the other social networking tools they use. We can also install basic internet filters to stop our children going to inappropriate websites that may distort their view of relationships (e.g. violent and pornographic sites) and encourage self-destruction (e.g. anorexia and suicide sites). There are some free filters around — K9 is one — which are easy to download and set up.

The big message here about technology is to protect our children for as long as possible while they live with us. That means remaining vigilant

— not anxiously so, but enough to help them live a balanced life where the internet can benefit them and where using the internet is just one of their activities. Any more than three hours a day online is probably too much in my book, but this is an individual preference. We actually don't yet know the what the effects of more than two hours' use each day might have on children's development, but what we do know is that their internet usage — including the use of phones — should not come at the expense of them sleeping properly, learning at school, enjoying face-to-face time with their friends and family, and leading balanced and healthy lives. There are some very good articles on children and technology on the Raising Children website (see resources pages). Why not organise for one of the authors here to speak at your school?

resources and further reading

BOOKS

Allen, D. (2001). *How to get things done: The art of stress-free productivity*. Ringwood, Vic.: Penguin Books.

Colvin, G. (2008). *Talent is overrated: What really separates world-class performers from everybody else*. London: Nicholas Brealey.

Covey, S. (1989). *The 7 habits of highly effective people*. New York: Simon & Schuster.

Doidge, N. (2008). *The brain that changes itself: Stories of personal triumph from the frontiers of brain science*. Melbourne: Scribe.

Faber, A. & Mazlish, E. (2001). *How to talk so kids will listen & listen so kids will talk*. London: Piccadilly Press.

Goleman, D. (1996). *Emotional intelligence: Why it can matter more than IQ*. London: Bloomsbury.

Gottman, J. (1998). *Raising an emotionally intelligent child: The heart of parenting*. New York: Simon & Schuster.

Heininger, J. & Weiss, S. (2001). *From chaos to calm: Effective parenting of challenging children with ADHD and other behavioral problems*. New York: Perigee Books.

Latta, N. (2010). *Politically incorrect parenting: Before your kids drive you crazy*. Auckland: HarperCollins.

Patterson, K., Grenny, J., McMillan, R. & Switzler, A. (2008). *Crucial confrontations: Tools for resolving broken promises, violated expectations, and bad behavior*. New York: McGraw-Hill.

Patterson, K., Grenny, J., McMillan, R. & Switzler, A. (2005). *Crucial conversations: Tools for talking when stakes are high*. New York: McGraw-Hill.

Patterson, K., Grenny, J., Maxfield, D., McMillan, R. & Switzler, A. (2007). *Influencer: The power to change anything*. New York: McGraw-Hill.

Peck, M. Scott (1978). *The road less travelled: A new psychology of love, traditional values and spiritual growth*. New York: Simon & Schuster.

Phelan, T. (2010). *1-2-3 Magic: Effective discipline for children 2–12*. 4th ed. Chicago: ParentMagic Inc.

Pickhardt, C. (2003). *The everything parent's guide to positive discipline: Professional advice for raising a well-behaved child*. Cincinnati/New York: F+W Media.

Roeder, M. (2010). *The big mo: Why momentum now rules our world*. Sydney: ABC Books.

Shore, R. (1997). *Rethinking the brain: New insights into early development*. New York: Families and Work Institute.

Siegel, D. (2009). *Mindsight: change your brain and your life*. Melbourne: Scribe.

Siegel, D. & Hartzell, M. (2004). *Parenting from the inside out: How deeper self-understanding can help you raise children who thrive*. New York: Tarcher/Penguin.

WEBSITES

The Australian Centre for Education in Sleep (ACES) <www.sleepeducation.net.au>

Joachim Posada says: Don't eat the marshmallow yet. TED.com <www.ted.com/talks/lang/eng/joachim_de_posada_says_don_t_eat_the_marshmallow_yet.html>

Mental Stillness <www.mentalstillness.org>

Parenting books and DVDs <www.parentshop.com.au>

Raising Children Network <raisingchildren.net.au>

Sleep Health Foundation <sleephealthfoundation.org.au>

acknowledgments

I dedicate this book to my mother, Anne, who is alive and well, and my father, Richard, now deceased, for the warmth and love they gave me and my brothers (Paul, Chris and David). My parents provided us with a warm and loving family life. In our early years, our family was a place for us boys to thrive and feel confident to take up life's challenges.

To my wife, Simone, and our lovely children — Dom and Isabelle — I acknowledge your patience with me these past two years in covering for me when 'life got hectic' as I was writing this book. Simone, you in particular have been a pillar of strength in many ways — quite apart from your support of me in writing this book.

To my staff at Parentshop, Vicki and Astra, thank you. To my advisers June Gibson, Angela James, Nicky Wallington, Wim DeVylder and Bob Green, thank you for your encouragement. All of you have kept me focused on putting something together to make a difference to the lives of families. To my colleagues Annette Flanagan, Jules Ober, Jenny Gunderson, Brad Williams, James Brown, Brett Drinkwater, Michael and Rebecca Lines-Kelly, Jacki Short, Stephen Luby, Terry Laidler, Greg Legg-Bag, Peter Chown and Tom Phelan, you have given me your time in mentioned and unmentioned ways.

I also acknowledge the contribution of the now thousands of family professionals we have trained and who work with parents day in and day out. You are in many ways the unsung heroes in family life and your stories have added to the colour in this book. You are the 'parents in lieu' of parents who lack a closer connection with their own families.

To my editors, Emma Driver (fastidious, intuitive and adroit — I'm not the first to say this) Jane Curry and Sarah Plant, and my illustrator, Martin Chatterton (a funny and contemporary picture craftsman), I say thank you.

index

ONLINE PARENTING COURSES
with www.michaelhawton.com

With *Talk Less, Listen More* — online — you will see:

- Three key rules for working out your job as a parent
- Expert video clips of psychologist, Michael Hawton, who explains the benefits of the *Talk Less, Listen More* approach
- Easy-to-follow whiteboard illustrations to complement his online teaching
- Animated examples of parenting strategies — the ones that tend to work, and some that don't!
- Opportunities to try out what will work for you at your place — PDF worksheets and a scenario quiz

To find out more scan the QR code or go to www.michaelhawton.com and follow the prompts to online courses

letter to professionals

This book is a hands-on guide that has been designed to help readers look at their own family situation and to make changes to their lives with the help of a therapist or on their own.

As a professional you can use *Talk Less, Listen More* to reinforce skills you teach to clients and to continue what they are learning after they have visited you. The information, worksheets, diagrams, summaries and quiz enlist the clients' participation to use what is learnt in counselling to everyday life. The steps in the book are taught sequentially, with each chapter building on the previous ones. One way to use this book is to have clients read parts of the book between therapy sessions to reinforce what you teach them.

Talk Less, Listen More can be purchased in bookstores throughout Australia, New Zealand and the United Kingdom. In addition, some clinicians have opted to order multiple copies of *Talk Less, Listen More* to make the book readily available to clients. For details on our volume discounts, see the *Talk Less, Listen More* order form under the order forms tab at www.michaelhawton.com